Amigas
RISING

LIFTING OTHERS AS WE CLIMB

Compiled by
Esmeralda Aharon y
Gabriela Ramírez-Arellano

Amigas Rising
Lifting Others as We Climb
Esmeralda Aharon and Gabriela Ramírez-Arellano

Published by Latinas Rising, LLC, O'Fallon, MO

All contributing authors to this anthology have submitted their chapters to an editing process and have accepted the recommendations of the editors at their own discretion. All authors have approved their chapters prior to publication.

Project Management and Book Design: DavisCreativePublishing.com
Cover Design: Missy Asikainen
Writing Coach and Editor: Jacqueline Duty

Publisher's Cataloging-in-Publication
Names: Aharon, Esmeralda, compiler. | Ramírez-Arellano, Gabriela, compiler.
Title: Amigas rising : lifting others as we climb / compiled by Esmeralda Aharon and Gabriela Ramírez-Arellano.
Description: O'Fallon, MO : Latinas Rising, LLC, [2025] | In English with some Spanish phrases.
Identifiers: LCCN: 2025907760 | ISBN: 9798991398725 (paperback) | 9798991398732 (ebook)
Subjects: LCSH: Hispanic American women--Social conditions--Literary collections. | Hispanic American women--Psychology--Literary collections. | Self-esteem in women--Literary collections. | Leadership--Literary collections. | Mentoring--Literary collections. | Power (Social sciences)--Literary collections. | LCGFT: Self-help publications. | BISAC: SELF-HELP / Motivational & Inspirational. | SELF-HELP / Personal Growth / Success.
Classification: LCC: E184.S75 A45 2025 | DDC: 305.48868073--dc23

ATTENTION CORPORATIONS, UNIVERSITIES, COLLEGES, AND PROFESSIONAL ORGANIZATIONS: Quantity discounts are available on bulk purchases of this book for educational, gift purposes, or as premiums for increasing magazine subscriptions or renewals. Special books or book excerpts can also be created to fit specific needs. For information, please contact **Esmeralda Aharon, Latinas Rising, LLC at hola@latinas-rising.com, and https://latinas-rising.com/.**

I am celebrating the powerful women in this anthology. Together, step by step, they have carved out personal lives and business environments that lift others. As the CEO and founder of Acumaxum, being part of Amigas Rising *has been an opportunity to connect with new communities. This anthology amplifies women's voices as they share their stories of resilience, leadership, and impact.*

—DEBI CORRIE, CPA, CGMA
CEO and Founder, Acumaxum, LLC

Amigas Rising *has given me an opportunity to reflect on my life and realize all the lessons learned that I can pass on to those around me. I am blessed to be part of this fabulous, inspiring group of women!*

—JACLYN NOROÑO-RODRIGUEZ, MBA, CPSP
#1 International Best Selling Author of
Calladitas Rising: Reclaiming Your Power, Strength, and Voice

Being part of Amigas Rising *has been an empowering journey of sister-hood, storytelling, and lifting one another higher. This transformative experience has connected me with incredible leaders, mentors, and change-makers whose stories are must-reads!*

—LINDA ROBINSON
Award-Winning Community Leader

I'm thankful for all my women of color and identities that truly make me an edge walker of many cultures in my world. I'm especially thankful to be in the company of so many great women in this Amigas Rising *anthology. It is a literary kiss over my own lifetime pilgrimage!*

—CHAPLAIN (MAJ) LISA NORTHWAY, U.S. ARMY
Family Life Chaplain

Being part of this anthology affirmed that our lived experiences are powerful tools for transformation. I feel honored, seen, and inspired to continue helping others unlock their own voice and purpose.

—VERONICA SORIA, ED.S., M.ED., M.A., ACC
CEO, MVS Solutions LLC

Amigas Rising: Lifting Others as We Climb *is a master class in networking with impact. My new amigas are allies, advocates, and amplifiers, ensuring consejos/lessons learned are shared widely to create an informed and powerful leadership tribe within the Sisterhood.*

—LISA CARRINGTON FIRMIN, Award-Winning Author
CEO and Founder, Carrington Firmin LLC
Colonel, USAF Ret.

It is truly an honor to author my own story of women's empowerment, love, and strength in the anthology, Amigas Rising: Lifting Others as We Climb. *This collaborative project raises voices and amplifies the importance of sisterhood.*

—GABRIELA OCHOA, BASC
#1 International Best Selling Author of
Calladitas Rising: Reclaiming Your Power, Strength, and Voice

DEDICATION

Para Mi Madre,
To the first woman who taught me how to rise:

Vestida de fuerza y dignidad,
con sabiduría en tus labios y bondad en tus manos,
me enseñaste a caminar con fe y a levantarme con valor.

This anthology of sisterhood and rising
es para ti, mi fuerza, mi raíz, mi inspiración
cuyo legado siempre será
mi llamado a brillar and to lift others as I climb.

Con todo mi amor,
Esmeralda Aharon

For Adriana, who helped me find my voice
when she asked, "Why are you here?"

And Victor—*Sin miedo al éxito, todo lo puedo gracias a tu apoyo.*
Thank you for supporting every big, bold dream…even the ones
that make no sense at all.

To those who see me, lift me, and cheer me on:
May we all keep rising, *juntas,* with purpose, power, and love.

Gabriela Ramírez-Arellano

TRIGGER WARNING:
Several chapters in this book describe the authors'
experiences overcoming the effects of
personal and professional trauma, including
sexual assault, suicidal ideations,
health adversities, grief, and the effects of war.

TABLE OF CONTENTS

Continued on next page

Foreword

Amigas Rising: Lifting Others as We Climb is a multicultural collection that crosses many bridges of understanding, and it resonates deeply with me. I was very honored to be asked by Gabriela and Esmeralda to write the forward of this second book in their series. As a former international exchange student, I developed a deep appreciation of what it means to be a newcomer in a community and to lean on the strength of other people who invest in helping others rise.

I clearly remember spending a summer living with a family in France that did not speak any English, which was challenging and pushed my French language skills. The family had one young daughter, so I became the "older sister" of the family. This sharpened my knowledge of what it feels like to be the newcomer in a community, to learn new norms, and to grow.

This experience of global culture deepened when I returned home and my family began hosting dinner guests through the World Affairs Council, welcoming international visitors who came to our city. My sense of being a global citizen grew. These early experiences instilled in me a desire to mentor international colleagues and minorities who were rising behind me in the corporate ranks during my business career. Although I was among the first women rising in corporate America at that time, I was committed to bringing others along with me. I also benefited from mentors who guided me on my path. I knew women around the country who had already risen to higher levels of corporate success, and they were willing to share their wisdom with me.

My background with international businesspeople and local civic engagement led me to become the founding executive director of the St. Louis Mosaic Project. The goal of the St. Louis Mosaic Project was to make our region the fastest-growing major metro in the country for growth of the foreign-born population. We accomplished this! The word "Mosaic" represents an art piece composed of many colorful pieces forming a whole, which symbolizes all of us, not only international people in our community. The second book in this series reflects that vision beautifully. *Amigas Rising* shares the stories of Latinas, as well as other women in our community who are creating a movement of lifting others as they climb. At the same time, the authors in this book see and reflect the warmth of the community that Gabriela and Esmeralda are building. This warmth extends not only among the contributors but beyond our borders thanks to their previous anthology, *Calladitas Rising: Reclaiming Your Power, Strength, and Voice.*

Our multicultural community is increasingly expanding past our region and even our national borders. Data demonstrates the increased importance of the Latina population in the U.S. and in St. Louis, across the arts, social services, education, business, and government. We are witnessing not only an increase in numbers but also a rise in leadership from this diverse demographic. *Amigas Rising* is a powerful way to increase visibility of the talent represented by Latinas and others who are committed to global voices. The authors show both their competence *and* confidence by sharing their stories and pathways to success.

Each story in the book highlights a woman's path and her strategy. By showing both the story and the strategy, this format helps readers recognize that advancement, whether in life or career, requires intentional and strategic effort. Some of the stories show how new doors have opened for the co-authors when other doors closed, revealing the resilience and adaptability of these women. I believe this book will open further pathways for its authors, as readers across the country and around the world seek them out for new opportunities.

My hope for you, the reader, is to appreciate the gift of each story from these authors who share their paths with you. May these narratives inspire you to one day share your own story in the future so other women coming along will benefit from your journey as well.

—Betsy Cohen
Philanthropic Futurist
FutureGood (www.WeAreFutureGood.com)

Betsy Cohen was a corporate executive at Nestlé Purina and the executive director of the St. Louis Mosaic Project. She is now a philanthropic futurist with FutureGood consultancy. She is on the external board for Washington University McDonnell International Scholars Academy, the St. Louis University Chaifetz Business School Executive Advisory Board, and the advisory board for CEdge consulting firm. She is the author of a book to help international people find a U.S. job and a TEDx speaker. She is a graduate of Wellesley College and has her MBA from Harvard Business School.

Esmeralda Aharon

Rise and Shine, *Mija*

The title of this anthology is rooted in the powerful aspirations of a visionary woman, Mary Church Terrell, who believed in the collective advancement of women. An American educator and civil rights activist who lived from 1863 to 1954, Terrell was a founding member and the first president of the National Association of Colored Women (NACW) established in 1896. Alongside trailblazers such as Harriet Tubman and Ida B. Wells, Terrell helped shape the enduring slogan: "Lifting as we climb." This motto embodied their belief that the progress of one woman should pave the way for the advancement of many. Their work was never about individual success, but about forging a collective path forward, an ethos that still resonates just as powerfully today.

With that incredible legacy in mind, and surrounded by *amigas* from diverse cultural, professional, and spiritual backgrounds, it felt only natural to frame this anthology in the same spirit of solidarity and service. Just as the NACW's purple and gold banner boldly proclaimed, "Lifting as we climb," the cover of this book carries that legacy forward through its purple and gold floral design, symbolizing royalty, justice, and spirituality. We added pink to represent femininity, softness, gratitude, and respect. This is a gentle reminder that strength and tenderness can and do coexist within us.

Like the founding women of the NACW, the co-authors of *Amigas Rising* have not only risen through adversity but, in the spirit of "Lifting as we climb," have turned around to uplift others. Though our stories come from women of many cultures, professions, and life experiences, they are united by a shared ethic of resilience, compassion, and collective purpose. This collection honors the legacy of Mary and the women of the NACW, whose vision of communal advancement continues to inspire across generations and backgrounds.

Through this anthology, it is my most profound honor to help amplify the voices of these *amigas*, each one living proof of the power of rising together and of the beauty of collective success. Like them, I have lifted others as I climbed, starting from my earliest memories. Growing up in a Spanish-speaking home, I became the translator for my mother, interpreting everything from school documents to my report cards. (Thankfully, I was a good student and did not mind reading my grades aloud!) This early sense of responsibility became the foundation for how I lead, serve, and love people today with empathy, compassion, and conviction.

Later, as an Air Force chaplain assistant, I had the privilege of walking alongside service members, their families, chaplains, first sergeants, and commanders, helping protect their First Amendment rights of freedom of religion. Across two decades in the Chaplain Corps, I poured my heart into leading, mentoring, and guiding Airmen through moments of triumph and heartbreak, helping them find strength and purpose. I ministered to families, offered worship services, facilitated rites and education, and provided a safe space for healing and hope, which often refueled the spirit for the mission ahead. In those quiet, sacred moments, I learned that true leadership means lifting others, not just in faith but in life, while honoring the incredible diversity of beliefs that make our military community so rich and resilient.

During one deployment after September 11th, I witnessed service members quietly weeping while speaking with their families, some from homesickness, others from heartache. As I waited to call my own family, I prayed silently for their strength and comfort. One young Airman, who lived in the same tent where I bunked, was going through a painful breakup. Her muffled cries at night reminded me of the women who cried in the darkness during basic training. Just as I had then, I gently approached her, offered comfort, and shared words of hope. This same Airman is now married and has a beautiful family. These conversations remained confidential and holy, and, in those moments, I was not just serving; I was lifting.

In recognition of my service to God and country, I was deeply honored to receive the prestigious Spirit of the Four Chaplains Award. My friend and colleague Sue Busler is steady, strategic, and unwavering. She saw something in me long before I could name it myself. That is what sponsorship looks like: lighting the flame in someone else.

"As a chaplain assistant, Aharon has had the privilege of working with officers and enlisted members of every denomination. All have been positively impacted by her professional work ethic, her confident leadership, and her vast knowledge, to say nothing of her kindness, empathy, generosity, and selflessness" (Busler, 2011).

Yet even this distinguished recognition pales beside the true privilege of having lifted countless others, both in uniform and beyond. The Holy Spirit, ever present in my life, made it clear: I was not meant to rise alone, and uplifting others with service, courage, and conviction has guided every chapter of my life.

As I shared in previous anthologies, my faith has long compelled me to act on behalf of others. "Speak up for those who cannot speak for themselves, for the rights of all who are destitute" (Proverbs 31:8, NASB).

This verse became my compass as I transitioned to my current role at Saint Louis University School of Medicine, where I support faculty, staff, and learners in cultivating a culture of dignity and belonging. In this new mission field, my ministry continues through the lens of social justice, which I have come to see as sacred work.

My divine leader, Jesus, commanded with presence. He sat with the brokenhearted, broke bread, and listened deeply. He drew people in. His was sacred leadership: knowing when to advocate, when to hold space, and to see everyone with the eyes of God. Luke 4:18-19 records Jesus' first public message, quoting Isaiah: "The Spirit of the Lord is on me, because he has anointed me to proclaim good news to the poor...to set the oppressed free." This scripture was not only a spiritual proclamation but a direct call to action for social, economic, and systemic justice. Jesus consistently reached out to those excluded from society, such as the poor, women, the sick, tax collectors, lepers, Samaritans, and even enemies. "...Whatever you did for one of the least of these brothers and sisters of mine, you did for me" (Matthew 25:40, NIV). This ethic of care is foundational to social justice work today, emphasizing dignity, inclusion, and compassion.

Mary Terrell embodied this type of leadership. A champion of racial justice, women's rights, and educational equity, she used her voice not to overpower but to elevate. Her legacy teaches us that empathy, courage, and conviction can transform not only systems but souls. Social justice, in her hands, was not only resistance to oppression but a deliberate act of restoring dignity, advancing equity, and building a more humane world, work our time desperately needs. Like in Terrell's lifetime, racial inequities are still deeply embedded in our institutions, manifesting in disparities in education, healthcare, housing, and wealth. The ongoing struggle for voting rights echoes the very battles she waged over a century ago, as new legislation and systemic barriers continue to suppress marginalized voices. Much like Terrell faced resistance to women's full participation in public life, today we witness attacks on women's autonomy, access to reproductive healthcare, and fair representation in leadership. The racial terror and violence of her era may not wear the same cloak, yet it resurfaces in modern forms of brutality, hate crimes, and mass incarceration. Her call to "lift as we climb" resonates urgently now, reminding us that progress requires courageous, persistent, and collective action against the forces that still seek to divide and diminish humanity.

Mary's life reminds us that leadership is most powerful when it lifts others from the shadows of doubt into the light of their potential. That truth came alive for me in a deeply personal way, not in a courtroom or on a protest line, but in a book club where one conversation became a turning point. Let me tell you about a moment that changed both a student and me. She was a first-generation Latina medical student, anxiously preparing for her residency interviews. Her shoulders slumped beneath the invisible weight of self-doubt. Though her voice spoke professionally, her eyes whispered the question so many of us have silently carried: Do I really belong in medicine? Others circumvented her question, focusing on logistics. But the Holy Spirit stirred within me, moving me to respond with grace, wisdom, and empathy. I leaned in and reminded her of all she had already overcome and of how proud we were of her. She hesitated, then quietly confessed: "I feel like I am playing a role. Like I am going to be found out." That was doubt speaking a lie rooted in the systems of oppression that try to silence the brilliance God placed within her and us.

Looking into her eyes, I said, "You belong here! Not only have you checked every box, but you are exactly what medicine desperately needs. It needs your culture, your background, your language; it needs you. Your future patients will feel your compassion in every gesture and know they are truly heard in every word you speak." Tears filled her eyes, and I simply held space for her at that moment. Weeks later, she graduated and stepped boldly into her residency, carrying that truth with her. She wrote to me:

*"I honestly look up to you so much…You are such a strong woman
who always keeps going for more, and you have shared those opportunities with me. I really want to thank you for that." Dr. Jennifer Villa*

That, *amiga*, is the true heart of rising together: discerning when
someone begins to shrink and to speak life back into them. Be the friend
you wished you had, the one who shows up in their doubt and celebrates
in their joy. This is the legacy Mary gave us: not a climb to the top alone,
but a rise that takes others with you. Authentic leadership does not simply
reach heights. It changes lives and transforms communities. Mary did
that for us!

Therefore, rise, *amiga*, not only for yourself, but for the sister
watching from the shadows, wondering if she belongs. Let your light
blaze a trail she can follow. Rise because healing is holy, because courage
ripples outward, and because the world needs women, ready to lead with
faith, empathy, courage, and bold purpose. "Let your light shine brightly
so others may see your good works" (Matthew 5:16, NIV). Shine so boldly
that the next generation never feels the need to dim their light to belong,
in the military, in the university, and in the fight for justice and equity in
every space they enter. You are not only rising; you are lifting people who
will one day rise higher because you chose to light the way.

Let me close with the words I shared at the inaugural "*Si Se Pudo*"
Latine pre-commencement graduation ceremony at Saint Louis University:

*"Our community has faced challenges, yet we rise. You are gradu-
ating in a year that has tested you in every possible way. You have
lived through political debates that question your belonging. You
have shown up when showing up was the hardest thing to do, with
moments of isolation in spaces that were not always built with us
in mind. Some of you crossed oceans of doubt to be here…Yet you
rose! Let me remind you: You are not here by accident. You are here*

because your ancestors dreamed of this. Your abuelos and abuelas worked the fields, cleaned homes, crossed borders, and sacrificed everything so that you could one day wear this cap and gown. Today, their wildest dreams walk across this stage. You have shown the world that Latino excellence is not a trend, it is a legacy, and you are that legacy. As you go into the world, remember your voice matters. Your culture matters. Your story matters. Whatever you become, bring your whole self with it. Do not shrink to fit into systems; reshape the systems. Break ceilings, build bridges, and never forget where you came from.

This moment is not just about you. It is your lineage. Whether you show up in heels, in botas militares, in Crocs, in chanclas, in whatever makes you whole, you made it. You are a graduate, a trailblazer, a story of resilience in motion. Against all odds, you rose! You are your ancestors' answered prayer.

To your parents, my respects! They prepared the sandwiches at 5 a.m. They said, "Sí se puede, mijita, mi hijito," even when they did not know how. They prayed, cried in silencio, and gave everything so this day would come.

Class of 2025…keep dreaming audaciously. Lead unapologetically. Remember the tears, the joy, the struggle, the triumph. Use your degree like a machete: cut through barriers, create pathways for others, and stay rooted in your values. Wherever you go, remember you belong in every room. Your voice matters in every conversation. You were not just born to survive; you were born to lead!"

To you, *amiga*, I say: Rise like the founding women of the NACW, who saw the injustices around them and refused to stay silent, believing that the progress of one woman should pave the way for the advancement of many. They used their voices to elevate others, not overpower them, and to demand social justice where there was none. You, too, can sponsor others just as my friend and colleague did for me when she nominated me for the prestigious award for walking alongside others in moments of injustice or their darkest hour. Shine so boldly that the next generation never feels the need to dim their light to belong in the military, university, or in the fight for justice and equity in every space they enter. *Brilla* so fiercely that no one coming after you must ever question whether there is a place for them at the table. Because you, *amiga*, are not just rising, you are lifting, lighting, and leaving a legacy of faith, empathy, courage, social justice, and action that generations will follow. Finally, as the co-authors of *Amigas Rising* will show in their narratives, we rise through adversity and, in the spirit of "Lifting as we climb," we resiliently turn and lift others too. Now rise, and shine, *Mija*! The world has been waiting for your light to lead the way. Yes! Together, we rise higher, stronger, and unstoppable!

Esmeralda Aharon, M.A., is a speaker, international best-selling author, mentor, and co-founder of *Latinas Rising LLC*. She is the embodiment of resilience, faith, and purpose. A first-generation American born near the U.S.-Mexico border, she overcame poverty by working as a migrant farmworker before joining the United States Air Force. Over 26 years in Religious Affairs, including 20 months deployed to the Middle East across four tours, she walked beside service members and their families, helping them find spiritual resilience. After retiring from the Air Force, Esmeralda became a champion for social justice, advocating for healthcare equity, language access, and opportunities for women veterans. Today, as program director at Saint Louis University School of Medicine and a doctoral student in higher education, Esmeralda continues to live by the ethos of "Lifting as we climb," using her voice to open doors and inspire generations to rise.

Please scan the QR code to connect with this author.

Gabriela Ramírez-Arellano

The Power of One

When I moved to St. Louis in 2016, I wasn't sure what I was walking into, but I knew I wasn't walking alone. My husband, Victor, and I got married in 2014, and when he shared his dream of opening his own restaurant in Missouri, I said yes to the adventure. At the same time, my mother was struggling with her health, and the pull to be closer to family cinched the decision. That move was a leap of faith, a mix of dreams, responsibilities, and the hope that we could build something new together and start over.

From the beginning, Victor gave me something few people ever had: permission. Permission to dream big. To fall. To fail. To rise again. He has never asked me to play small. His steady belief in me gives me the courage to say yes to the things that once scared me. We were both starting over, and neither of us knew where it would take us.

Still, the road forward wasn't easy. In 2012, I went through a divorce that made me question my identity, my worth, and my place in the world. I had to unlearn the lies I had been told and the ones I told myself. I believed lies that said I was too late, too broken, too small. I am grateful I didn't stay in that place. I couldn't.

Edward, Adriana, and Marcela were watching me. They needed a mother who didn't give up; who showed up. One who could fall and still rise. One who could face the fire and still lead with love. I realized then that I wasn't just rewriting my story. I was showing them how to write their own, and I refused to let our story end in brokenness. I didn't get it all right, but I gave it my all and showed them that resistance is in the getting up again and again. After my divorce, I signed up for a business class through the ProsperUS Detroit program because I wanted to learn how to start something of my own. I wasn't looking to lead; I was looking to make ends meet, but life had other plans, and in the process, I was reminded of my superpower—speaking Spanish.

Not long after, I was asked to create the curriculum and begin teaching and coaching small business owners in both Spanish and English. *Me.* The woman who had just begun to believe in her voice was now being asked to amplify the voices of others. I stepped into it scared and unsure, but I stepped in anyway. That experience changed my life and the lives of many in that community. It taught me that leadership isn't about having all the answers but rather about standing in the space and saying, "Let's figure it out together."

I thought that divorce was my breaking point, but grief came next and cracked me open completely. In 2020, I lost Edward. In 2021, I lost Marcela. There are no words that make sense for their loss. I was stripped bare. In that silence, in that emptiness, I realized I had nothing left to lose. That's when I began to say yes to everything that once felt too big: speaking, building, mentoring, taking up space, dreaming out loud. The grief didn't disappear, but when I made space for it to breathe, it gave me clarity. Saying yes reminded me there is more to feel than just the ache. Suddenly, the things that scared me weren't so scary anymore because I knew what hitting rock bottom felt like. I had survived it, more than once, but not by myself. My siblings showed up in that season and never left. They sat with me, held me, and reminded me of who I was. That kind of support is quiet and sacred. Through it all, Victor remained that steady strength nearby, giving me space and comfort. He has been a soft place to land and a mirror when I forget my worth; never pushing, but always present. His dream brought us to St. Louis, but his love gave me permission to live the life I always dreamed of.

From that place of pain and purpose, I stepped slowly but fully into the work I was meant to do. Eventually, I joined Cortex, continuing my work to expand access for small business owners and changemakers. This work has allowed me to walk alongside entrepreneurs who, like me, are trying to build something meaningful. This role has given me a front-row seat to the resilience of our community, our region. Building and convening have deepened my commitment to making sure as many people as possible have access to opportunity, regardless of where they are starting.

Everything I have worked toward has been with one mission in mind: to give others a chance to see themselves fully, in their greatness. Because I know what it feels like to doubt, to not be included, and go without. Because I will never forget what that felt like, I use every platform I have to open doors for others. My focus is on building bridges to help others see what's possible, even when it's hard to envision. When someone sees your potential and gives you the tools to grow, everything can change.

My focus has never been on titles or accolades. It's about creating belonging. It's about mentoring, sharing the mic, and lifting others. It's about making introductions and opening doors, especially the ones people don't know they're allowed to knock on. If I have access, I'm sharing it. If I know a name, I'm passing it on. That's how we rise together.

What I wish more people knew is this: *your* power is real. Even when you feel unseen, even when you are starting over or falling apart. You still carry power, and the most beautiful way to use it is to see someone else's.

Reach back. Make room.

Never underestimate the power of one.

The power of one person to change a life.

The power of one decision to change a direction.

The power of one intention to create a ripple effect of transformation. I was that one. Now, I challenge you to be that one.

Be the one who doesn't wait for permission.

Be the one who makes the call, starts the project, and lifts someone up.

Be the one who turns pain into fuel and dreams into action.

Because this world doesn't need more perfection, it needs more real people.

More builders. More cheerleaders. More people who say, "I have been through it, and I am still here. Let me help you, and let's do this!"

**Together, we rise.**

Gabriela's journey, from Mexico to the United States, has been deeply influenced by her immigrant experience. Her commitment to making a difference isn't just a choice; it's an intrinsic part of her being, a way of paying forward the support she and her family received, and a way of championing causes that are greater than herself.

Returning to St. Louis in 2016, Gabriela embarked on a mission to uplift small businesses, foster economic growth, and ensure language access. Her work at Cortex and the BALSA Foundation reflects her dedication to empowering entrepreneurs in underserved communities and building strong local business relationships. Her impact has been recognized with honors as a Diverse Business Leader, a Woman of Distinction, an Influential Business Woman, and a Woman of Achievement.

Gabriela's passion for elevating bilingual Latinx voices led to the creation of the *Auténtico* Podcast and We Live Here *Auténtico*, platforms that amplify stories and inspire others.

Through her work, including co-founding STL *Juntos* during the pandemic and Latinas Rising in 2024, Gabriela honors her children, Adriana, Marcela, and Edward, who drive her work to create a better world.

Please scan the QR code to connect with this author.

Mirna Therrien

From Silence to Strength

My story is told with honesty, vulnerability, and a deep desire for healing. It's not about blame. It's about breaking the silence that held me hostage for years. The people in this story are real. Some I still love deeply. This is not about exposing people; it's about exposing pain and reclaiming my voice.

For years, I lived in survival mode. I gave everything; my body, my time, my voice, my dreams, to others. I served my country in the Navy, built a family, and worked tirelessly to help fellow veterans. On the outside, I was strong. Inside, I was disappearing. I didn't believe I mattered. That lie lived deep inside me from childhood wounds, military trauma, and years of emotional neglect. It took a moment of complete collapse for me to cry out to God: "Please, I can't do this anymore." That was when the healing began.

The Roots of Silence

I joined the Navy young and hopeful. I wanted to serve with honor. Early on, I was sexually harassed and later assaulted. When I reported it, I was silenced and retaliated against. The message was clear: Stay quiet if you want to survive.

One senior leader believed me and transferred me out quietly. He couldn't undo the harm, but he gave me a lifeline. Still, I buried the trauma and kept moving. I smiled through the pain. I didn't know that burying it would nearly bury me. My body began to break down. I developed fibromyalgia, chronic fatigue, IBS, PTSD, migraines, and later ankylosing spondylitis and osteoporosis. I lived with invisible wounds, barely functioning, still believing I had to be strong. I didn't know that strength includes softness. I didn't know that rest is holy. I didn't believe I was allowed to ask for help.

God Interrupted My Silence

While stationed overseas, a woman invited me to a Christian women's retreat. I didn't go for spiritual reasons; I went for a break. During worship, something supernatural happened. A woman I'd never met called me forward and spoke truth over my life. They were things she couldn't have known unless God had revealed them. She saw my pain. She called out my gifts. I wept uncontrollably. For the first time, I felt seen. Not for what I could do, but for who I was.

I remembered a moment in Navy boot camp, standing frozen on a diving board. I couldn't swim, and I believed I would drown, but when I jumped, something shifted. I didn't drown. God carried me. That image came back again and again. It was more than a memory. It was a metaphor: You didn't survive because you were strong. You survived because I carried you.

Motherhood and the Breaking Point

Years later, I married and gave birth to a miracle daughter. I'd been told I might never conceive, but God gave me a dream of her before she was born. Holding her felt like holding my heart outside my body. She was my joy, my reason to keep going. As life got harder, I began to shrink again. In my marriage, I felt unseen. Decisions were made without me. My voice was dismissed. I was the caregiver, the planner, the fixer, but

I was never invited to just be. I performed for love. I gave until I had nothing left.

Eventually, my health collapsed. I could no longer work. My identity was shattered. I was forced into early retirement from the VA, where I had worked as a social worker helping veterans. I felt like I lost everything: my job, my worth, my purpose.

In 2023, I made the most painful decision of my life. I stepped away from everything familiar: my marriage, my child, my old patterns of self-abandonment. I stepped away, not because I stopped loving them, but because I had to learn how to love myself. I knew if I didn't, I wouldn't survive, and I wanted more than survival. I wanted to live.

How I Dove Into Healing (Step-by-Step)

Healing wasn't a magic moment. It was a thousand small choices:

1. **Therapy**—I began trauma-informed therapy with a specialist who understood PTSD, military sexual trauma, and complex grief. I faced the pain I had buried for decades.

2. **Faith-Based Recovery**—I joined Bible studies, inner healing prayer groups, and attended spiritual retreats for women dealing with deep emotional wounds. I learned that God doesn't shame us—He restores us.

3. **Community**—I connected with safe, empathetic women who had also walked through trauma. We held space for each other's stories. We cried. We laughed. We healed—together.

4. **Body Work**—I explored somatic healing practices, including gentle movement, massage therapy, and breathwork, to reconnect with my body in safe ways.

5. **Creative Expression**—I began writing again. I journaled. I wrote poetry. I shared parts of my story at veteran gatherings and women's conferences.

6. **Boundaries**—I stopped saying yes to things that drained me. I learned to say no, even when it was uncomfortable. I no longer apologize for taking up space.

7. **Mentorship**—As I healed, I began mentoring other women veterans and survivors. I spoke truth to them as it was spoken to me: You are not too broken. You are becoming whole.

Helping Others Heal

Today, I use my story to serve others, not from a place of perfection, but from lived experience and deep empathy. I mentor women veterans, survivors of sexual trauma, and anyone navigating the heavy burden of invisible wounds. I lead workshops on reclaiming identity, boundaries, and soul restoration. I walk with women who feel like they've lost themselves.

Now, as a certified mental health life coach, I offer personalized support to help others:

- Reconnect with their true identity
- Break cycles of shame, silence, and burnout
- Create boundaries rooted in self-respect
- Heal from trauma through faith-informed tools and practical steps
- Find joy, purpose, and peace in their lives again

If you're reading this and you feel like your voice has been buried, know that you're not alone. Healing is possible. Wholeness is possible, and you are worthy of both. You don't have to stay stuck in survival. I'm here to walk with you toward strength.

You matter. You are enough. Your story is not over.

A Letter to My Daughter

My *Chula*,

You are my heart, my joy, and my answered prayer.

I know my choices in recent years have caused confusion and pain. I want you to know this: I never walked away from you. I walked away from a version of me that couldn't show up for either of us.

I needed to learn how to be whole. Not just for me, but for you. I didn't want to keep teaching you that love means self-erasure. I didn't want you to grow up thinking that your needs are too much, or that being a woman means always giving while receiving nothing in return.

You deserve to see what a healed woman looks like. Not perfect. Not always strong. But honest. Present. Free. You are not responsible for my pain, but you were one of my greatest motivations to heal. I want our bond to be built on truth, not performance. I want you to know that your voice matters. Your dreams matter. ***You*** matter.

I love you more than words can hold. I'm here, fully, not as a shell of a mom, but as a whole woman who is still growing, still healing, still becoming. I am so proud of you. Keep shining. Keep asking questions. Keep taking up space, and never, ever forget:

You are seen. You are chosen. You are deeply loved.

Love always,

Mami

Final Words

My story is still being written. There are still days of grief, doubt, and fatigue, but I am no longer silent. I no longer live to please. I live to be present, to be real, and to be free. If you are reading this and feel broken, invisible, or forgotten, I want you to hear me clearly: You matter. You always have. You always will. This is the most important truth I've learned:

- You don't have to earn your worth. You were born with it.

- You are not too broken. You are becoming.

- You don't need to shrink. You were made to rise.

Here I stand—not because I have all the answers, but because I finally understand the question: Who told you that you didn't matter?

That voice was a lie.

You matter. Your voice matters. Your story matters.

And so does mine.

Mirna Therrien is a proud U.S. Navy veteran, licensed master of social work, certified life coach, and first-generation Latina who has dedicated her life to helping others heal from trauma, reclaim their self-worth, and break the cycle of unhealthy relationships. With a deep understanding of generational wounds, military culture, and the complexities of identity and belonging, Mirna brings both compassion and clinical insight to her coaching and therapeutic work.

Through her practice, she empowers women—especially other first-generation Latinas and veterans—to overcome adversity, rediscover their voice, and rewrite their stories. Her approach combines evidence-based strategies with culturally-informed care, guiding her clients toward emotional resilience, healthy boundaries, and personal freedom.

Mirna is also a highly sought-after speaker and advocate for mental health awareness in underserved communities. She continues to promote healing spaces where individuals can turn pain into purpose.

Please scan the QR code to connect with this author.

Catherine Baez

Coqui Dreams and Bagel Mornings

Where does my story begin? Sitting back and reflecting on my life and journey, I have had to ask myself that question repeatedly. What story do I want to tell? How do I even start it? As a true Nuyorican (this is the term used for someone living in New York with parents from the island who honor its traditions), I am the youngest daughter of a Puerto Rican mother and a Dominican father. I reflected on my childhood and asked: Where does every good story and party begin in New York? In the kitchen, over some good *cafecito*, coffee talk, and a delicious plate of food.

During my writing process, I came to compare unpacking my story to a delicious pot of *Arroz con Gandules* that my mother would make, a simple dish of rice and pigeon peas. You start with oil, *sofrito*, add a pinch of salt, *sazon y adobo*, and all your traditional seasonings before you add your water and rice. Remember, never forget to wash your rice, which makes everything in that pot come to life. That one simple pot, with all these delicious flavors of fresh cilantro, peppers, onions, and garlic simmering together, brings generational traditions to life. These simple ingredients unite families and friends during holidays and special occasions, sharing stories from the island of Puerto Rico to the struggles in New York, yet we all continued to see the beauty and richness in our lives while blasting traditional *merengue* and *salsa* music. This is how I have decided to bring my story together. I plan to write with tons of love for storytelling, community, and an appreciation for how a simple life can surprise you with bursts of flavor, color, unplanned moments, excitement, and so many blessings simmering together.

Born and raised in New York City, I never gave it a second thought. I just assumed everyone was from New York. My mom moved to the Big Apple when she was 16 years old, leaving behind the beautiful island of Puerto Rico that she loved so much and would always say she would return to one day to open a school in her hometown of *Sabana Grande*. Little did she know that her plan wouldn't unfold as she had dreamed. Waiting for her was an older gentleman, a family friend from Puerto Rico, who, at first sight of her, asked for her hand in marriage, forcing my mother into an arranged marriage. All her dreams were then stripped away, and she found herself with two kids, married to a man who was not a kind, gentle soul. Eventually, she became close friends with community leaders and some powerful women who were part of the Young Lords and Black Panther movements. These women helped my mother break free and find her path to working for the New York City schools.

Now a single mother, she wanted to focus on her original plan, but little did she know that her Dominican neighbor had plans to introduce her to her son, who was traveling from Santo Domingo to Brooklyn, New York. It was a mutual attraction, and with my dad's *papi chulo* swag, she let her guard down and decided to take a leap of faith in love. Their love story led to my sister and me, which many call Irish twins because of our close age difference of about a year and a half. I became my mother's shadow, cherishing every moment I spent with her. Time with her felt like a movie; she would stop time when she entered a room, her smile lighting up wherever she went, and people were always drawn to her and charmed by who she was. Her gentle laughter and her caring nature, especially toward children, were beautiful traits that I wanted to emulate.

My mother taught me to embrace my *Latinidad* and New Yorkness while leaning into being my authentic self and finding my support team, a team that doesn't judge, as we should never judge others because we all have our own stories and journeys. Speaking English and Spanish, or rather Spanglish, at home created a dual world for me, one where I had to constantly switch codes, not just in language but identity. Celebrating Christmas Eve, also known as *Nochebuena*, with *lechón* and *aguinaldos*, then waking up for Christmas morning with a mixture of American and Caribbean traditions. Over time, I realized these weren't two separate worlds but rather two parts of the same rich story. Eventually, her love story came to a halt when she discovered my father had left behind a family in the Dominican Republic and was not living his truth. Once again, she found herself on a path she had never planned to be on.

Growing up as a Nuyorican and being blessed to live two lives, one in the Big Apple and the other on the enchanted island of Puerto Rico, was truly a blessing. This experience allowed me to appreciate all the beauty beyond my tough city. Spending summer vacations and every holiday on the island, Puerto Rico became my second home, a place I never wanted to leave. At times, I would beg my mom to let me stay with my grandfather. My mom would simply look at me and say she understood why I wanted to stay, but we had much to accomplish in New York, and if it was God's plan, we would all be back soon. We went back to the concrete jungle of New York, landing at JFK Airport, with tears streaming down my face. I felt torn between my love for a delicious slice of pizza, a warm cup of joe, and a New York bagel. Yet, I could still feel the Caribbean breeze on my skin, taste the delicious mangos and coconuts that had just fallen from the palm tree, and the precious sounds of the *coqui* singing me to sleep like a lullaby.

Returning to New York felt like stepping into a melting pot, an encyclopedia of cultures. I was fortunate to be surrounded by so many different families who came to New York seeking to achieve their dreams and find their voice. Raised by a resilient single mother who bounced back from whatever challenges lay in her path, she continued to support and inspire those around her, especially me. Growing up with a strong Latina mother wasn't easy. There were countless expectations both inside and outside the home. Sometimes the pressure felt heavy, but many say that the most beautiful gems are created under extreme pressure. I recall one of the first times I realized my voice mattered was in middle school when I joined the debate team, drama club, and wrote my first short play. Wanting to do more, I asked my mom for permission to volunteer at a local hospital and a senior living center, where many patients struggled with basic daily tasks. Here I was, a middle schooler eager to help others improve their quality of life. It fulfilled me and brought so much joy when they could feel like themselves again, experience normalcy, and regain hope that they could resume their lives. Seeing them smile and receiving a simple thank you from them or their visiting family members brought me immense joy.

One of the moments that defined me was being one of the very few Puerto Rican families growing up in Boro Park, Brooklyn, a predominantly Hasidic Jewish and Irish-Italian community, which presented challenges regarding identity and finding my voice in school and among friends. Taking the overcrowded New York City public bus to high school every day taught me valuable skills in navigating tough situations. I am grateful for the many lasting connections and friendships God has placed in my path during my early school years. Many of my friends and mentors are among the closest people to me, having become my family and inspiring me to stand firm in being my authentic self. At one point in my journey, I found myself in relationships that silenced my voice, as well as in my career, where it felt like I was allowed to be seen but not heard. I realized that the resilience my mother instilled in me was meant to help others, especially children, in finding their voices, helping those voices that were being silenced.

Before I found my purpose, I would have never thought that this Nuyorican would one day find herself in the Midwest, calling St. Louis her new home. I was beyond a doubt an East Coast gal making a Midwest shift. Moving there, I was fearful of the uncertainty and my doubts, but growing up in one of the toughest cities and experiencing a world change made me realize that life is precious, and we must be bold in the face of uncertainty. Arriving in St. Louis, I only knew two people I had visited twice before, but never in my wildest dreams did I see myself creating a beautiful life for my daughter and me, filled with friends who are like family and opportunities I had only dreamed of. The first few months in St. Louis were the hardest. I missed the constant hum of the city, the smell of fresh bagels, and even the rhythm of the New York streets.

Building on that foundation of faith and resilience, it is these special relationships and bonds that God has gifted me with that confirm this was the right choice, and I am so grateful. All the individuals I have been blessed to be surrounded by have helped me see that I want to empower those voices, using a theater stage, a classroom, book readings, and being part of a community of like-minded people who have found their voices and helped me to find mine. I continue to remind myself that life doesn't always go as planned, and being okay with that shift is important. Leaning on one of my favorite scriptures, Jeremiah 29:11, reminds me how God has a plan for you that is bigger and greater than you could ever imagine for yourself. I hold onto my dreams of being the voice for the voiceless within education and communities, helping children find their voices and letting them know silence is not an option.

Looking back now, I am living my dream, doing it because I love it, and my journey shifted me to the Midwest. I realized that your dreams can come true no matter where you are. Moving from the East Coast to the Midwest with my youngest daughter and my beloved four-legged companion, Pumpkin, meant stepping into the unknown, knowing that sometimes you just have to lean into your faith and trust in the process of a plan you would never have thought possible, a plan that can result in the most beautiful painting. You can step back and gaze at it because of the unexpected beauty of all the colors that make up this life you are now living. What once felt scary and unpredictable has now turned into a colorful painting that you will continue to gaze at with amazement and gratitude.

Now, when I sip my *cafecito* in St. Louis, I taste all the stories my mother carried, the dreams she planted in me, and the voice I was always meant to use, not just for myself but for every child who still waits to be heard.

Catherine Baez is a Dominican-Puerto Rican educator and passionate advocate for arts and education. Originally from New York, she brings over 15 years of experience in special education and theatre instruction across both New York City public and Charter schools.

In 2021, seeking a better work-life balance, Catherine relocated to St. Louis—a move that inspired her to pursue her Ph.D. and led her to embrace the city as her second home.

Beyond her academic journey, Catherine works closely with students and families throughout St. Louis County and City, raising educational awareness and supporting young people in achieving their academic goals. Her unwavering commitment to educational equity and youth empowerment is deeply rooted in her belief in the transformative power of community.

Actively involved in local initiatives, Catherine plays a key role in uplifting and uniting the Latino community in St. Louis. A lifelong theatre and arts enthusiast, Catherine seamlessly blends creativity, cultural pride, and inclusivity into everything she does inside the classroom and out.

Please scan the QR code to connect with this author.

Debi Corrie

The Unlikely Entrepreneur

My journey to entrepreneurship was not a typical one. It was filled with successes and failures. Prior to starting out as a business owner, I was a C-Suite executive. I had no desire to own my own business. I saw how hard business owners struggled and did not wish that upon myself. These people worked hard and nonstop. I enjoyed being an employee. Besides that, I had a couple of side hustles. I had a Mary Kay business that I started in 2012, which led me to meet Kris. She and I started a tax practice and had Mary Kay consultants as tax clients. That business, which was only for vacation money, became Taxpertise, a boutique tax firm with just under 100 clients. Life was good, and being an employee was job security.

2015 was a significant year for me. I worked for a startup company that had international offices and was working eighty hours per week. I had no work-life balance. During that year, I began to look at entrepreneurship differently. After a year, at the age of 54, I came home one day and told my husband that I no longer wanted to be a W2 employee. I was going to start my own business.

My husband asked me if I had lost my mind. What he did not know was that it was actually his fault. When I was looking for a job this time around, before I decided to start my own business, my husband said something that was incredibly eye-opening to me. He asked me why it was that once I got things fixed up, I wanted to leave. "You've already gotten through the difficult part. Why wouldn't you stay when everything is fixed?" This was the crux of my job problem. I had never really thought of the fact that I was someone who liked strategy and implementation. Once things were fixed, I wanted to move on. I did not want to do the day-to-day work. That wasn't for me. I like to work with the owner and visionary of a company to see their dreams succeed.

I joined a partnership that allowed me to have my own solo practice. I would not earn a salary, but run my own practice under the partnership. The partnership told me it took about six months to get your first client. They offered a support network for sales and networking. I thought, "They have a system. I can do this." I had no idea how hard it would be to get started.

If there was a way to do something wrong, I did it when I first started my business. When I started networking, I went to every event that I could. I gathered as many cards as possible. I made appointments to meet with as many people as possible. Needless to say, I wasn't having much success. One visit or connection was not enough to build trust.

My business coach taught me the importance of how to properly network and to give back. When I tried this approach, I might talk to two or three people at a networking event and ask lots of questions about them. I did not sell to them. People started telling each other to talk to Debi. **Lesson #1: Be a good listener, and you can get to know people on a deeper level.** These are the relationships that built my business.

One of the things I did at the partnership was talk to potential partners. I had been with the company for approximately three years and told one of the women candidates that she should talk to some of the successful women in the company. She could get a better understanding of what was required and what needed to be done to be successful. There was silence at the other end of the phone. I asked her if everything was

OK. She said, "Debi, I asked to talk to a highly successful person, and they sent me to you." It was a very humble moment. **Lesson #2: Acknowledge your success on the way to your goals.**

When the pandemic hit in 2020, I'd had my practice for four years and enjoyed my partnership, but I knew that I wanted to do business differently. Weeks before, I had joined a mastermind and coaching group, and my coach made me realize I could not reach my financial goals as a sole proprietor. The partnership did not allow for team members. We had to do all the work ourselves. To grow, I would need to build a team. If this were truly my goal, I had a tough decision to make.

If I wanted to be successful, I would have to go out on my own and have employees. This was a different model and was pushing me out of my comfort zone. **Lesson #3: Being brave is not about conquering your fear.** It's stepping into your fear and doing the hard things to be successful. If you are feeling that tingling in your stomach when you're trying to make a decision, it could be your gut telling you that it's time to get uncomfortable and make changes in your life.

In November of 2020, my company, Acumaxum, was born. I didn't know what the next chapter would bring, but I was ready to do business and life differently. That same month, I published my first book, *Loving Failure: Getting Control of Your Business Health.* My book was a lifelong dream. It was an international best-seller, and I celebrated this achievement with family, friends, and business friends.

Like any business owner, I was challenged with hiring the right employees and making sure that we had a successful business model. It took us a while to figure out who the right people would be on the team and what the business should look like. I have learned through failure what will work for us and what will not. For hiring employees, the number one requirement was to hire happy people.

In 2022, I got the brilliant idea to start accepting bookkeeping clients. Remember, we are a CFO company. I hired accountants to do the bookkeeping work, and then we started getting bookkeeping clients. The bookkeeping business was not working. I was making my people miserable. We were trying to do bookkeeping on a CFO model. It was broken, and as hard as I tried, I couldn't fix it. I had to let the bookkeeping business go. It was hard; it was a failure. We stopped accepting new clients and refocused on our CFO business. For the first time in 2023, our business did not grow but remained flat. We had to retool and get refocused on what we were good at.

Success includes a lot of difficulties. You must be able to enjoy the small victories and not wait to enjoy success until you get to the top of the mountain. You will never be satisfied with the life you are creating if you only let yourself enjoy the end goal. What I have learned on this journey is that, as women, we tend to forget that our biggest asset is ourselves. We are the only people who can protect that asset.

Here are some other lessons I have learned along the way:

Never sell me short. My price is my price, and the right clients are willing to pay it. If you are an employee, the same is true. Know your worth and make sure you get it. If an employer is unwilling to pay what you are worth, it is time to move on. I did that at least two times in my career.

Share your story. Men share their stories all the time, and that's how they learn from one another. They share their business stories and their successes. As women, many times we are taught that this is boasting, and we are being arrogant. It simply is not true. Sharing your story gives permission and inspires other women to share because they can point to your story. They will say, "If she can do it, I can do it." You may help them strive for a new goal or dream.

As a recovering perfectionist and control freak, **I am letting go of 100% and living by the 80/20 rule**. I am not a perfect mom, wife, or business owner. I am a magnificent work of art that is also a work in progress. My imperfections are what make me a good human.

Stop comparing yourself to others. Like me, you are on your own journey and your own timeline. The only person that you need to be accountable to is yourself. Learn to like what you see and change what you do not.

Never stop learning. The world is an ever-evolving place. Be open to new things. Pick what works for you and learn to say no to the rest.

You control your narrative. Stop saying you aren't enough. You are an amazing human. Accept a compliment graciously. (That means just say thank you; nothing more.) Acknowledge that you are a work of art in your own right.

At the end of the day, **it is family and friends that matter the most**. Make sure to make time for the things that are important to you.

Do something crazy this year that makes your stomach tingle. It will work or it will not, but you will know the answer. When 80-year-olds were asked what they regretted most when they looked back at their lives, it was the path they did not travel because of fear. Now they wonder what would have happened. They regretted not taking more chances. Have the courage to take chances and live your best life.

Debi Corrie is a business owner and CEO of Acumaxum, a strategic CFO company. Her firm specializes in helping companies improve cash flow, increase profits, and scale their businesses. She is the author of *Loving Failure: Getting Control of Your Business Health.* The book focuses on helping business owners understand how to use numbers to build successful companies. She tells stories and gives pointers for new startups and experienced business owners.

Debi is a strategist, board member, and public speaker. She owns three other businesses: Taxpertise, LLP; DJC Media, LLC; and SheLed Badass Podcast. She is the recipient of the Gateway to Dreams Impact award for 2019 and recognized by the *St. Louis Small Business Monthly* as a Top St. Louis Business advisor for 2020 and a Titan 100 recipient in 2023. She supports women's and children's causes that lift people up.

Please scan the QR code to connect with this author.

Venus Martz

Venus

Happiness is not the goal. The journey, the lessons, the connections we create, the connections we break, and the connections that heal us give life meaning and wonder. Looking from the outside in, people may think I've got it all together. I've had a successful career so far. I'm well-educated, well-rounded, and for someone living away from their home city, I could be seen as well-connected. On paper, with accolades achieved and charity work that I've volunteered for, it's pretty good being me.

What no one sees is the woman who constantly reminds herself to get up. I have to remind myself, "I can do hard things, I have done hard things, I have come from hard things."

The success of my life is the reflection of my mother. She is my namesake, my lifeblood, and undoubtedly the most difficult and stubborn woman I've ever known. My mother wasn't thrilled to find herself pregnant with me. She already had five children and didn't want another burden to carry. She was so worried that I'd be problematic that she prayed to God for a well-mannered and good-hearted child, and if that's not who I was going to be, He could have me back.

That night, she had a vivid dream that revealed a daughter who would love beautiful clothes, perfumes, and have a joyful personality. God also imparted to her my name, the exact timing of my birth, and the details of my arrival into this world.

On the morning of Wednesday, October 10th, 1984, I—Venus Twinkle—was born in the city of Manila, Philippines. True to her prayers, I was joyful and well-mannered. Even as a young child, I easily laughed and was particular about what I wanted to wear and how I wanted my hair to look. My mother got the daughter she requested, but she would only have a few short months to mother me when I was born.

In her early thirties, she and my father embarked on a journey to America from the Philippines, pursuing the elusive "American Dream." Aware of the potential for failure, she embraced the challenge with immense determination, refusing to succumb to defeat. She knew her goal, she saw the challenge, and she was focused on what steps she needed to achieve them.

Even before I was born, they would travel back and forth by visa, trying to find someone to sponsor them to immigrate to America. They had to prove that they would be useful immigrants, that they were hard workers, that they wouldn't be burdensome to society, and above all, that they could pay their way into the country.

That's what they did. They developed a plan and found friends who would help them along the way.

At just 36, my mother faced the heart-wrenching choice of leaving her infant daughter in the care of family friends in the Philippines to chase her dreams or surrender the hope of the "American Dream." She chose to continue. She knew that one day it would be worth it, that the pain of leaving me would one day lead the way for my success in a country full of possibilities.

When I was seven months old, she packed my brothers and sisters and moved across the world, leaving me with family friends, praying for the best and believing that this short-term sacrifice would be worth it in the end.

They struggled for many years. My siblings would be split up for months, sometimes years, staying with different family members in New York and other parts of the country. They relied on the kindness of friends. Using the little resources they had, they accepted any help they could get along the way. At one point, my sisters lived in Louisiana with friends, while my other sister lived in New York with our grandmother. My mother reunited them in Ohio, and they lived in a trailer that was provided by pastor friends. Life wasn't easy for my family.

My mother worked odd jobs here and there, and my father, a minister, would be away for months at a time, preaching across the country. They starved; they were separated from each other just as much as I was separated from them. At one point, my oldest sister, at around 13 years old, had to deal with the landlord because my mother couldn't face him again to tell him that she didn't have enough for the rent.

After years of struggling, my parents became naturalized citizens of the United States of America, and they settled in Staten Island, New York. And after seven years of petitioning the Philippine government, I was finally able to reunite with my family. My mother fulfilled her endgame of having us all together in America.

When I arrived in New York City, I was hit with the cold, bitter winds of springtime. As I stepped out of the airplane at JFK Airport, I landed in another world. I had only ever met my parents; they would come once a year, for a few weeks, to visit. This was my first time meeting my siblings, all five of them.

I wasn't sure if these strangers, who shared my DNA, had any genuine affection for me. I remember standing in the living room, with its maroon carpet, mirrored walls, and floral sofas, wondering if this was truly where I belonged. My siblings hugged and kissed me, and it felt both strange and comforting at the same time. My mother cried tears of joy, finally having her baby back, which was what I had longed for, yet it also made me feel sad.

New York was the first time I heard real arguing. I once woke up to my parents fighting about money. I was so impressed because even their fights were in English and not in our native tongue of Tagalog. They didn't speak much Tagalog at home; everything was in English, and we were submerged in the American, albeit New York, culture.

No sooner had I settled in New York than my father decided to leave us. Two years after I finally immigrated, my father abandoned us for another woman in the Philippines. He then spent the rest of my childhood to adulthood traveling back and forth. Sometimes he'd stay in New York for six months, sometimes we wouldn't hear from him for a year. At times, the only real news we'd hear about him was rumors that his mistress was pregnant, or some new, shocking scandal. He traded being a husband, a father, and a pastor of a church in New York City to be a businessman in the Philippines, parading his mistress as his new wife to parishioners and erasing us.

I still remember my mother getting a certified letter in the mail, going into her room, shutting the door, and not hearing from her for the rest of the day or night. She opened an annulment request from my father. I can only imagine the devastation that washed over her. Here, her husband, the father of her six children, was requesting an annulment. Divorce was one thing; it meant there was history. Annulment nullifies every shared detail of their marriage; it erases the children she bore, the life she endured, and the woman she was. The Philippines does not have divorce; it only annuls a marriage.

She was in her mid-40s when she received that annulment request. She never signed it.

She was in survival mode. The time for catering or empathy as a mother was gone. She was suspicious of everything and everyone. Our "I love you, Mom" was often met with: "If you love me, keep my commandments!"

We would be woken up at 6 a.m. for family devotions and watch our mother cry out to God in the corner, asking why He had given her such horrible children. We sat there, quiet, internalizing her words and wondering if they were true. Realizing she was breaking down.

I can look back with empathy knowing that she was grieving the death of her marriage, the erasing of her womanhood, her strength, and her dignity. She was in her forties, going through menopause, hemorrhaging, going to work, trying to feed her children, alone in New York City, the only adult in a room full of innocent children. This 5'1, Asian woman, with a dream of America, was the only one standing between her children and starvation.

For many years, she was the ground that we walked on to fulfill our own destinies. Her life was not happy, and that wasn't her goal. It was for her legacy to survive and her dream to be fulfilled. She looked at the challenge and faced it head-on. Maybe she was scared or fearful, but she never let that change her course. She had a plan. She knew leaving me in another country was heartbreaking, but staying would be soul-crushing. She acted; she didn't sit by and let life happen to her. She took life by the throat while it thrashed and kicked. Wounded and scarred, my mother made plans, sought help, used what little resources she had, and succeeded. And although she had her own mental breakdowns, she was in constant prayer and was in a constant state of gratitude.

On harder days when I have doubts, I write down all the things that I've done that I didn't think I could do, then I write down a list of things I need to do and the steps I need to take to achieve them. One by one, even when I'm afraid, even when I don't think I can, I tell myself: "I can do hard things, I have done hard things, I have come from hard things."

My mother single-handedly raised six kids, lifting us into lives that turned out to be successful, empathetic, kind, God-fearing, and hard-working. We are her American dream. Her fingerprints are all over the lives we lead; our children are the legacy of her tears, hard work, and an often loveless and bitter life.

On her deathbed, riddled with the pandemic and cancer, she was full of joy. She lived long enough to see her dream fulfilled and on Zoom, with all of her children together, near and far, she lifted her hands and prayed a benediction over us: "May the Lord God bless thee and keep thee, may the Lord God shine His face upon thee, and be gracious unto thee, may the Lord God keep His countenance upon thee and grant thee peace."

Thank you, Mom!

Venus Martz earned her Bachelor of Arts in Communication from Lindenwood University in St. Louis, Missouri. With over 15 years of experience in economic and business development, she has successfully managed projects from the early design and planning stages through to implementation, achieving positive impacts and measurable results. Venus specializes in creating effective campaigns and events with specific goals and objectives, tailored for diverse audiences and various organizations, including both private corporations and non-profit entities.

As a philanthropist and committed community member, Venus has been an active board member for several organizations, including North County Inc., Valley Industries, St. Martin's Child Care Center, the Emerson YMCA, and Walter's Walk. She has also volunteered for numerous organizations, such as the Saint Louis Crisis Nursery, BJC Christian Hospital, the USO, and the City of Florissant's Economic Development Council.

In recognition of her contributions, Venus was named one of North County Inc.'s 30 Leaders in Their Thirties in 2017, included in *Small Business Monthly's* Top 100 St. Louisans to Know to Succeed in Business in 2018, and recognized as one of the *St. Louis Business Journal's* 2023 40 Under 40.

Please scan the QR code to connect with this author.

Lisa Carrington Firmin

The School of Firmin

I know what it is like to not have a role model: to not have anyone who looks like me or is even of my same gender in the room with me, much less as a mentor, a boss, or a sponsor. I didn't work for a woman until I had been in the military for eighteen years, and that was at the Pentagon. It never happened again until a few years into my career in higher education. I have never worked for someone with my own ethnicity. I know how isolating that can be, so I made it my mission to help others, to mentor and sponsor those with potential and talent. There are so many out there who just need an opportunity, not a handout.

Professionally, I set a tough pace with my work ethic as a military officer, Bronze Star-decorated combat veteran, commander, higher education professional, entrepreneur, founder, author, and poet. I refer to myself as a reformed workaholic who sometimes relapses, more often than I care to admit. Admittedly, it is hard for me; I am an extremely driven Latina who uses my *ganas* to make a difference in my life and the lives of others. I strive to balance between always going full steam ahead and pacing myself.

My work centers around helping others, especially women and veterans who endured traumatic experiences. I want to share the wisdom and healing I've learned with as many as I can. I suffered while climbing the ranks…endured sexual harassment, sexual assault, gender and ethnic discrimination, and misogyny. Why should they suffer? I lifted others as I climbed, and now I *pull* others up so they, too, can enjoy a fulfilling and successful life.

I've mentored many men and women throughout my career in the military, higher education, and entrepreneurship. For a long time, they would reach out to me only when they needed help or guidance in a particular demanding situation. They needed someone they trusted to provide family talk with brutally honest feedback that we sometimes need but can be afraid of.

Prior to my first command in the military, I drafted my leadership philosophy and shared it with all my direct reports. Most were astounded that their leader did that, especially my civilian staff. Most had never experienced a leader who was so transparent. My intention was to inform them of how I led, what I expected, so they could never not know where they stood. I believe in giving folks the parameters of my leadership style and then setting them loose to execute their way, as long as it is legal. I am known to say that I am never going to jail for anyone; I will never compromise my integrity or ethics. I don't tolerate those who do.

At that first command, a brand-new second lieutenant arrived. Late. Married. Expecting a child. His military orders were precise. We expected an unmarried officer on time. He was a mess. Great intentions but terribly executed. I took him under my wing, showed him my leadership philosophy, and began an uphill mentoring effort.

Frankly, I had my doubts about his judgment, decision-making ability, and talent. I stuck with him and mentored the hell out of him. He did have talent, but desperately needed guidance. He became a sponge and, in time, became an officer I was proud to say I had mentored. He went on to become a lieutenant colonel in the Air Force. He would email or call me every time he got promoted to thank me. With my leadership philosophy in his office, he would reflect on it and ask, "What would Firmin do?"

Going full circle, that was my first command, and in my final command as an Air Force ROTC Commander, I helped a young student garner three waivers so he could join the ROTC program at The University of Texas at San Antonio (UTSA). This enabled him to participate in the program and get a commission as a second lieutenant. He graduated as the first in his family to finish college and went on to become a lieutenant colonel. He had the talent; he just needed the opportunity.

This newly minted second lieutenant reached out to me every time he got promoted, got married, and had children. He also kept my leadership philosophy and all the lessons I taught him close. To say I was proud of both officers would be an understatement. When a mentor gets this kind of feedback on a continuous basis, they are doing something right, making a positive impact.

I recall one occasion where a young officer reached out to me asking for advice on how to handle a supervisor who constantly undermined her efforts. This young officer was still angry when she called me and wanted to respond emotionally. I talked her out of that and helped her see a better way, using facts and professionalism to respond to the situation. In time, the supervisor came to see just how smart and innovative the young officer was.

Competence is the key to success. I baffled my naysayers with excellence. I never gave anyone a reason not to promote me, always remaining professional. That is the lesson I shared with her. What joy and satisfaction I felt when she notified me that she had been selected for command and promoted to lieutenant colonel. I burst with pride at her and all my mentees' accomplishments.

I updated that original leadership philosophy over the years to include adapting it to the higher education environment where I found myself in post-military service. I continued to mentor those with talent and provide opportunities. First, as an associate provost for Faculty/Student Diversity and Recruitment, where I founded the UTSA Top Scholar program, and later as an associate vice president of the UTSA Veteran and Military Affairs department, which I also founded.

In an adjunct role as the UTSA representative for the UT System Women's Senior Leaders Network, I asked a particular professor who moderated a panel I served on if she wanted to participate in the network's leadership program. I saw talent in her and wanted to sponsor her as my protégée. I explained that the program focused on pairing protégées with sponsors who could advise and open doors to opportunities. The first thing she said was that she wasn't a leader and never envisioned herself as one. It should be noted that she didn't say I couldn't be a mentor or sponsor to her because I wasn't faculty. Leadership is leadership. I have been fortunate in being able to transfer my skills to any environment I find myself in. I guided her and lifted her up to others. Most importantly, I believed in her. She later became a college dean. Talent is everywhere; one just needs the opportunity to showcase and further develop it.

A sponsor does so much more than a mentor. They speak up on your behalf even when you are not in the room. They open doors to increasingly competitive positions and stretch assignments. However, women remain over mentored and under sponsored. I had no idea that I had a couple of sponsors when I served in the military until years later. They advocated for me among senior leaders, and several of my high-profile positions were directly related to them doing so. I was always capable, but in a handful of cases, they ensured I had the opportunity.

Several individuals in higher education referred to my leadership philosophy and expertise as The School of Firmin (TSOF) and proudly declared themselves graduates, citing my leadership to others. My military mentees have joined in with this and say they are also proud graduates.

There are at least two higher education graduates who say they are the first ever TSOF distinguished graduates. Who can argue with them? They are wicked smart Marine veterans with PhDs.

Now my mentees reach out to me to let me know of a promotion or other important career milestone and of the joys they've found in their personal lives, much more than they ask for help. I've even collaborated with a few. This brings the mentor/mentee relationship to a whole other level. The mentees appreciated that I took a chance on them and helped change the trajectory of their lives positively. I will never forget the few sponsors I had in the military and how their intentional actions did the same for me.

Speaking of trajectories, I need to state just how strongly I feel about lifelong learning and education. I was the first person in my family to get a college degree, which completely changed my life. I set up an endowment, the Colonel Lisa Carrington Firmin Scholarship, at my alma mater, Texas A&M University-Kingsville, for military-affiliated first-generation students. I want to help others earn their college degrees. I am an avid reader and enjoy learning new things; this type of intellectual curiosity is important as a leader and as an individual.

I use my gifts to make transformational changes, as I did as the founder of the UTSA Veteran and Military Affairs department and the UTSA Top Scholar program. I am doing it as the founder of my business, Carrington Firmin LLC, and with my Latina Warrior™ trademark. I am a storyteller who writes, speaks, and provides consulting in leadership, writing and authorship, veteran culture, transitions, military sexual trauma (MST), and intersectionality.

My books are another way that I make a difference. I traded in my body armor for the power of the pen. As an author, I believe that I have contributed to the dialogue on MST and how one can heal from PTSD, MST, and combat-related trauma. The two books I have published, *Stories from the Front: Pain, Betrayal, and Resilience on the MST Battlefield* and *Latina Warrior,* along with all my other publications, are examples of making an impact. I own my narrative and document it for the historical record, alongside the many stories I've written of others' journeys.

An anthology of prose, poems, and art chronicling my journey, *Latina Warrior* is an autobiography done in a deeply personal, sometimes humorous, intense, and explicit expression. I didn't hold back and revealed my authentic self. I wrote about the horrors of war and the PTSD that followed me home, of the sexual assault I endured, a divorce after many years, the therapy and healing journey I'm still on, but I also wrote about the joys of my Latina culture. It allowed me to have tremendous post-traumatic growth. I was honored to have Major Christina Helferich-Polosky (US Army ret.) illustrate the 50 poems in the book.

I am working on my third book, about veteran entrepreneurs. I enjoy interacting with fellow entrepreneurs; the synergies and collaborations that occur are fulfilling. I'm blessed to have met veteran innovators and founders with powerful stories, who are allowing me the privilege of writing and sharing their entrepreneurial journeys. I write books, chapters, articles, and speak on topics that I am passionate about, stories that are not widely shared or hard to talk about.

By now, you can see a pattern in my professional life. The reformed workaholic in me struggles to throttle back. I want my life to have mattered, to be worthy of my blessings and place on the planet. My publications will live on forever. The impact I've made on others continues in the way they carry themselves and how they pay it forward.

UTSA dedicated a space as the Lisa Carrington Firmin Veteran Lounge on their large campus for veterans to hang out, study, and network. As the founder of their Veteran and Military Affairs department, this touched me deeply. Shield of Sisters named a legacy pioneer award in my name. The Shield of Sisters Lisa Carrington Firmin Pioneer award is presented annually to those making a difference and leading the way in helping sexual assault survivors and in the prevention of MST. I remain humbled and honored to have these named after me.

I didn't start out to leave a legacy like The School of Firmin; I started out just trying to make a difference, working hard and helping others. My legacy was cemented by doing the right thing even when no one else was around, by putting others first, by taking the tough road, by mentoring and sponsoring the generations that follow, by never giving up, by believing in myself even when others didn't, and by my words and actions. What an epiphany to learn that by living my life in such a way, I have forged a powerful legacy that continues to impact others. Stay tuned, I'm not done yet.

Lisa Carrington Firmin is a Latina, award-winning author, poet, and Bronze Star-decorated combat U.S. Air Force veteran. She is the author of *Latina Warrior* and *Stories from the Front: Pain, Betrayal, and Resilience on the MST Battlefield*, and founder of Carrington Firmin LLC. She also provides writing and consulting services in leadership, veteran culture, transitions, military sexual trauma (MST), and intersectionality.

Lisa retired from the U.S. Air Force as a colonel and its most senior-ranking Latina officer, after leading UTSA's AF ROTC program to the best in the nation. She has received many honors and accolades such as the Legion of Merit, the 2023 National Latina Symposium Veteran of the Year, UTSA President's Distinguished Diversity Award, United States Hispanic Chamber of Commerce National Latina Leader, Governor of Texas' Yellow Rose, National Diversity Council's Trailblazer and Most Powerful and Influential Women in Texas, Texas Diversity Council's Greater San Antonio LGBT Ally, Hispanic Women's Network of Texas Trailblazer, Distinguished Alumni from Texas A&M University-Kingsville, Community Service Award from National Society of the Daughters of the American Revolution, and Military Writers Society of America book award.

Please scan the QR code to connect with this author.

Lara Kern

Dancing in the Light

When a yoga teacher cues us to rise up into star pose, I'm going to be dancing. When they say, "You don't have to stay still here," I've already started moving because I didn't have to wait for the invitation. I'm not going to stand still. When they say, "Spread your arms and fingers open wide and take up space on your mat," I'm going to make movements that boldly embody joy and freedom and that help me feel like I'm showing up for myself. I simply refuse to not take advantage of a moment to shake it. It's something I often choose to do in many other yoga poses during practice, too.

I used to worry that other people in class would be thinking, "Who does she think she is?" Then I remembered that people are going to think what they want to think about you, so you should just go ahead and do what you want anyway. Then maybe it will inspire someone else to feel safe enough to do what they want to do, too.

A common theme of my life over the past few years is that people tell me that I'm a light. They've reached out to me on social media, saying that they don't know how I am able to glow so much, but they love to see it. They've watched me from the sidelines and notice how I seem different… happier. When this first started happening, I didn't know how to react. Of course, I recognized that I felt lighter and happier in more than one way, but impostor syndrome would grab the steering wheel. My thoughts would shift into first gear, of not feeling like I deserved to hear all the praise. Over time, I started to combat that response by whispering that quote about how "When you see something beautiful in someone, you should tell them." It would pop into my brain as my little reminder: "Well, they saw something beautiful in me and they told me, lifting me up. Isn't it about time I start believing it myself?" So I did. The journey to get there was one that required more than a fair share of both physical and mental subtle movements and wiggles in discomfort to finally take hold.

About five years ago, I woke up one day unable to move. To this day, I still vividly remember lying in my bed feeling like my body was on fire. It took all the strength I could muster to even lift my hand, arm, and elbow. Once I confirmed I was able to do that, I logically ruled out that I was paralyzed, although it felt that way. The amount of fatigue coursing through my body left me in a haze. I called for my husband, and he seemed to think I was just being dramatic. Being met with that response added even more fuel to the intense fire of pain I felt in my muscles. With his help, I managed to sit up in bed, and then it all went blurry, but the next thing I knew, I was sitting on the toilet. I couldn't quite position my hand to properly wipe the tissue paper to clean myself, let alone stand back up. There was nothing nearby to grab except for the wall. I roughly inhaled and grunted as I intensely struggled to pull myself back up to a standing position and then bend over to pull up my pajama shorts. Walking felt like how Bambi looked taking his first steps in the meadow, except I wasn't a fawn, and I surely wasn't surrounded by flowers. My feet and legs were incredibly puffy and swollen, and even now, recalling that sensation of the tightness I felt stirs emotions that I didn't even know I still had left to process.

The symptoms I just described weren't even the only ones I had already been experiencing, slowly over the past couple of years: hair loss, skin conditions, joint pain, TMJ, chronic headaches and migraines, panic attacks, unexplainable pains in my underarms and ovaries, facial and eye twitching. It all happened randomly at different times and never all at once. Doctor visits never provided me with answers. When I woke up to all of this that day in March of 2020, I started googling my symptoms, and I was worried it may have been MS. It took 10 months of constant doctor visits, testing, and specialist referrals while working with a physical therapist on Zoom calls during the pandemic to finally put me in a rheumatologist's office. After even more testing and an MRI, I received the diagnosis: seronegative rheumatoid arthritis. This meant certain markers don't show up in blood work, but it was enough to finally start treatments for this chronic autoimmune condition.

The tiny bursts of energy I started to feel again, along with the decreased inflammation, swelling, general fatigue, and pain, were slow at first, but noticeable enough to create excitement. Whispers of hope started crawling back into my thought patterns. Remembering all the work I had been doing with my well-established therapist regarding reframing statements quietly began to rekindle my light and will to live. After a couple of months of infusion treatments, I finally reached a point where I felt mobile enough to travel back to my hometown to visit my family. The pandemic travel restrictions had started to lift at the perfect time.

That four-week trip was the exact change of pace and environment I needed for it to finally click that thirteen years of staying in a toxic marriage (and enduring behavior that I shouldn't have allowed myself to endure in the first place) was long enough. We brought out the worst in each other. Staying in that relationship was killing me, as made evident by the severe autoimmune response of the physical manifestation of trauma. I made a move that I should have made long ago: I left. With the eager support and love of my family, who had long feared for my well-being, I abruptly relocated to my hometown. Spoiler alert: That sudden move set the tempo of the rapid rate of transformation that was to follow, and my life trajectory was forever changed in the process, as if signaling the universe that I was ready for anything.

At first, crying became a regular occurrence over the next few months as I started processing everything that had happened. I cried while going for long walks through the neighborhood park down the street. I cried while driving in the car. I cried in the grocery store and with my family and safe friends who let me verbally process through it all. At the time, it felt like I was taking up too much space. I felt as though I was too much, but everyone assured me they were there to hold that space for me. I slowly began to accept that all those tears were necessary. They were the overdue release of all the times I had previously held my tongue. They were the long-awaited side effect of all the times I had previously shrunk myself to fit someone else's demands to be…less. Once I opened myself to the idea that my tears weren't anything to be ashamed of, rather they were welcomed sparkles of liquid self-love streaming down my face, all bets were off.

I started noticing that I was speaking to myself in a much kinder, gentler way than ever before. Curiosity began bubbling up to the surface and helped me put the puzzle pieces together with the edges of the puzzle pieces acting as the cracks of a broken ceramic mug, where the light shines through—kintsugi. The voice in my head began to sound like a friend, which is when I made the startling realization that it was the first time it had ever sounded that way. This, in turn, acted as a catalyst for being more comfortable with speaking my mind to others. For the first time ever, I felt safe enough to say what was on my mind, externally. When I stopped silencing myself, I became the sound I'd been searching for, and once I got a taste for those words of assertiveness in my mouth, there was no turning the beat around. I wasn't OK with shrinking to stay small anymore, and I showed up differently in all of my relationships. It felt very unnatural at the start, like I was being sassy or rude, but I have since seen a quote that says, "The guilt you feel for setting boundaries is a sign of how deeply you were trained to abandon yourself." The way I felt that in my soul made it all click.

I went back to school for marketing, and it helped me hone in on how much I enjoy creating content on social media. I do that as part of my business service offerings now, and it fits this idea of training your inner voice. Treat your inner voice like the Instagram algorithm. What you feed the algorithm will, in turn, influence your feed. We are constantly sending our inner voice clues and messages about the content we want to see in our lives. If you don't like the content you're seeing, feed it different messages and search terms, because by golly, your brain is going to find patterns of evidence of whatever it is you feed it. Be kind to yourself in the process of training your own personal algorithm to the point that reframing negative thoughts becomes second nature. A split-second decision that you don't even think about anymore because it's just part of who you are. Before you get skeptical and trick yourself into believing it's not possible, I can assure you it is with mindful practice.

Seeing hope, light, and positive spin in any situation is a muscle that you have to learn how to flex to strengthen it, just like hours you can spend on a yoga mat flexing your body's actual muscles. It all comes down to the language you choose that helps you feel an affirmation to be true within your body. If it doesn't feel true when you say it to yourself, tweak the wording, or your own inner copy, if you will, until it feels true. This helps train your brain to rewire itself. Feeling the connection you make with your body in that moment is what helps you embody these affirmations and beliefs. Over time, they train your inner algorithm to filter the content you see in such a way that you naturally begin to gravitate toward different accounts to follow (and likewise unfollow) and different ideologies to subscribe to. The other glow-up phenomenon is that the strengthening of the belief and trust you have in yourself follows suit. Before you know it, you're manifesting the life of your dreams, but it all starts with those initial keyword change nudges—the baby steps, if you will.

Anytime I felt stuck along the way, I leaned into one of my favorite Emily Dickinson quotes, "Forever is composed of nows," and it helped me figure out how I wanted to spend that particular "now." We have so much more power over our circumstances than we initially think. Taking the tiniest of steps is better than taking no steps at all. And in those moments that you have to stay where you are, you might as well shimmy, shake, and give yourself permission to sparkle and shine your light.

The physical manifestation of momentum throughout all of this is when you embrace the importance of dancing. Sometimes, you can tap into the slow and subtle excitement that builds from celebrating the simplest moments of movement. When you lose the ability to move and think you might be dying, you, too, may never choose to stand still in star pose in a yoga class ever again. Seize the moment and accept the invitation. Now go, *amigas,* and dance!

Lara is a social media and image consultant, polyglot, yoga teacher, and Reiki practitioner who believes that how you energetically present yourself to the world matters. She helps individuals heal and build confidence through the power of fashion and self-expression, empowering them to step boldly into their authentic selves. Through social media marketing, content creation, and copywriting, Lara amplifies her clients' voices and brands, ensuring their message resonates far and wide. Equal parts free spirit and freelancer, she is a firm believer in the power of smiling at yourself in the mirror, has an eye for seeing the light in any given situation, and has a laugh that inspires laughter itself.

Please scan the QR code to connect with this author.

Maria Goncalves

Thriving Through Change

To my beloved children,

"We're moving to the USA in four months." Just like that, my stable, carefully built life began to shift beneath my feet. I was 39 years old, a mother of two, and living a very stable life in my comfort zone until my husband showered me with news that happened to change the second half of my life. I am from Portugal and, like most women in my traditional family, my name is Maria (Ines). With a bachelor's in political science and international relations, I worked as a people and business manager for more than fifteen years. I was the one who would never leave my country. However, the only certainty in life is that it is constantly changing, and so did mine.

Rooted in Strength

Let's rewind to the beginning of my relationship with change, when I was confident. I had it all under control with a confidence that only naïve, young, and inexperienced people can have. I was born in Lisbon, Portugal, in a traditional family. Conservatism mingled with freedom, open minds, creativity, and a lot of very strong women. My childhood memories are filled with the ballet/dance moves of my grandmother Dulce, the elegance and sophistication of my grandmother Josefina, the music played on the piano by my great-great aunt Margarida (I still see her fingers gracefully moving whenever I hear "Fur Elise"), the resilience of my physically weak great-aunt Regina who fostered more than 100 abandoned children. She provided them with shelter, food, education, and love. Also included is the forever young and free spirit of my mother. They were all strong, like-minded women who taught me the beauty of being a woman.

During my teenage and young adult years, I built some convictions. I wanted to be happy, free, and prosperous. I was committed to studying hard, investing in my career, traveling (for fun, and without ever leaving my country behind), and enjoying life. Being a mother, giving up on my career, or moving to another country was not an option for me. Life has a very particular sense of humor, don't you agree?

The Burnout

In my early 20s, I knew I was on track with my goals. I was working on my degree, and I had a great job. I was also teaching. I loved what I did and what I had. I had no clue that something I denied for my life could actually make my life even better and filled with purpose: motherhood.

When motherhood arrived in my life, I felt a sense of accomplishment I had never known existed. It was more than a life milestone, it was a nature call; it was an instinctive process, and the realization of both a kind of power and love that no reasoning or words can explain. My transition into life as a full-time professional, married woman, and mother of two was smoother than I anticipated. Until this moment in my life, I still felt like I had some control over my life. When you feel that confident, that's when life has other plans for you.

In 2011, my husband was offered a position to work abroad in several European countries. At the time, I had a solid career, two young children under three, and we had just moved from the city to the countryside to build our dream home. We decided he would travel for work and return on weekends, while I stayed in Portugal with the kids. I believed I could handle it all, as I always had. I was wrong. Suddenly, I was working 12-hour days, caring for two sickly toddlers, and managing a major construction project. After a year of this exhausting routine, I walked into my doctor's office late one day, with one child on each hip, a heavy backpack on my back, and desperation on my face. "What's going on?" the doctor asked. I crumbled. "I'm so tired, so, so tired…please give me some vitamins so I can keep going."

The physician knew I needed more than vitamins. That day marked a turning point. I was diagnosed with burnout and immediately placed on medical leave. I had a choice: start medication to manage my stress or drastically change my life to improve its quality. It didn't take long to decide. Taking pills to get through the day, having my kids be the first dropped off and the last picked up at daycare, recovering from constant colds and infections, and only seeing my children at bedtime because of a demanding job and no support—that was not the life I wanted. There is no judgment for those who choose differently. Every woman, every family has their own story, priorities, and limits, but for me, the hard choice was to leave my career and focus fully on supporting my family. I thought this decision would bring peace and relief. It didn't; at least not right away.

The Leap

During the following six years, I was a stay-at-home mom, which is not a typical situation. Never had I expected that, by choosing to support my family, I would be exposed to such an amount of judgment, bias, and prejudice. Those who hurt me the most, unexpectedly, were the ones coming from my closer circle. I was frequently asked how I would fill my days, how I would deal with boredom, how I would stay engaged in professional challenges, and how I would overcome intellectual setbacks. My ability to utilize my degree and career was also questioned, as was my ability to maintain my physical appearance. Initially, these unasked approaches would deeply hurt my feelings because they were so distant from the reality I was living in. Over time, I learned how to deal with these misjudgments, which lasted forever.

Over the course of six years, I supported my family, completed our dream house, managed some part-time projects, and built my resilience around dealing with other people's opinions. The differences in my choices did not match social modern standards. I knew I was looked at as different, and I found peace in my difference. Change found me again during this time of peace.

"We are moving to the USA in about four months." I was 39 years old, a mother of two, and living a very stable life in my very comfort zone until my husband showered me with the news that happened to change the second half of my life. I still remember closing the door for the last time and then watching the sunrise from the clouds before stepping into my unplanned *American Dream*. The days that preceded this move were filled with anxiety, crying, and uncertainty, but there was not a lot I could do except to, once again, support my family. That was the decision I had made in the past, and it remained my priority.

The Village

When I arrived in St. Louis, the first three to six months were exciting and busy. We were all trying to soak in the novelty. That thrill efficiently dribbled away any initial homesickness. Finding a new house to rebuild, experiencing a new and very appealing educational system, and being exposed to an engaging cultural part was exciting. Then, I reached the dreadful plateau of the expatriate spouses. My husband was successfully achieving his professional goals; my kids had settled into the new environment magnificently and barely needed me to translate their needs. Meanwhile, I was at home, having this new self of mine as company and trying to understand where I would fit in this new setting. I spoke broken English, had never worked in the USA, and had no friends. "It takes a village," they say. I did not have mine, and I struggled during an emotionally taxing adaptation process. I felt lost. I am aware that I come from a place of privilege (regarding where I was born, how I was raised, the place I had in society, and the life I was living). Suddenly, being seen as the outsider, the woman who dressed differently and spoke with an accent, made me feel exposed and vulnerable. I had to learn how to navigate change once again.

Unexpectedly, I got pregnant with my third child. Initially, that scared me even more. I was reaching my 40s, in a new country, and now, expecting a new baby. However, that pregnancy brought me so much grace, as well as a surprisingly supportive community of women who showed up for me, simply by knowing me from the neighborhood or my children's school. That was the first lesson America taught me: the power of community (something I lacked in my country when navigating a similar situation). I remember one day, my front door neighbor knocked on my door to let me know she was going to throw a baby shower for me. She knew I had no family support here, so she would take care of everything. I just had to provide her with my guests' names and enjoy the moment. I felt like crying. Still do. I also found immense support in the St. Louis Mom group, where I immediately became a contributing writer.

Becoming Whole Again

When my third child reached preschool age, I decided it was time. I had been fortunate to enjoy some years supporting my family, but I still owed myself the opportunity to be whole again, socially, culturally, and financially. Ten years had passed since I quit my career to support my family. I also owed St. Louis a chance. During this turning point, I set my goals. I would invest in myself and find my village, and so, I did.

In 2022, I registered for English lessons, won a project management scholarship targeting women returning to the workforce, and joined the International Spouses Group. Meeting other women in the same situation as I was helped restore my sense of belonging. Being able to support them helped me restore my feelings of purpose. I then joined the International Mentoring Program of St. Louis. This was the final support I had been looking for. Through it, I received mentorship from incredible people, learned about the American working culture, and finally put myself out there. I still remember one of my mentor's words before I attended my first (and only) job interview: *"Not everyone has technical skills, but everyone has a story, and you have a strong one that can take you wherever you want to go and thrive."* I listened, and I have engraved it in my soul to this day.

In 2023, my priority was to join a company with an international approach, and I could not have found a better one: LUZCO Technologies. LUZCO is a certified woman-owned business whose core values are diversity, leadership, and *familia*. I felt immediately embraced. LUZCO's vision and thoughtful leadership have allowed me to reembrace the workforce, restore my professional capabilities, and take them to another level.

In 2024, I launched The Portuguese Art Gallery with my family. This gallery has the dual purpose of invigorating business and showcasing the rich art of our beloved home country. I have also been granted the privilege of leading a group of mentees and mentors for the International Mentoring Program, where I simultaneously continue my journey of international engagement and contribute with meaningful connections and initiatives in the great city of St. Louis.

These experiences have enabled me to empathize with women who face the same struggles I did, support them, and help them find their way to success. Through every stage of this journey—motherhood, relocation, identity loss, and rediscovery—I learned that change doesn't break us. It reshapes us. I may have started as a woman who feared disruption, but I became one who thrives in it. Today, I carry those lessons with pride—not just for myself, but for every woman who has ever had to start over. I share them with my daughters and my son, so they know their mother did everything in her power to pursue joy, hold her family together, and grow with grace.

I have learned that doing what is easy can make life harder. Choosing the hard path, stepping into the unknown, following your truth, leads to a life of meaning, growth, and unexpected joy.

You can do hard things. Trust change. Find your village. And above all, enjoy the ride.

Maria Goncalves is a project management analyst supervisor, mentor, teacher, and writer whose journey reflects the power of resilience, reinvention, and grace through change. Originally from Lisbon, Portugal, a proud mother of three, Maria built a successful career in business and people management before choosing to pause professionally to support her young family. In 2017, she relocated to the United States, where she faced the challenges of starting over in a new country, culture, and language. Through perseverance and a deep commitment to personal growth, she reclaimed her professional identity and now supports other women navigating similar transitions. Maria is a mentor in international support programs and a proud team member at LUZCO Technologies, embodying the values of leadership, *familia*, and diversity. Her story is one of transformation, purpose, and the quiet strength that comes from choosing family, embracing change, and believing in new beginnings.

Please scan the QR code to connect with this author.

Patti Box

To Dream or Not to Dream

My dreams stopped many years ago. I had worked my way up to a good-paying job. Being an employee of companies for so many years, giving myself a little bump with each move, I felt like I had arrived. There were stressors involved, but more often than not, a payday wasn't one of them. I was blessed and thankful, but wasn't happy and fulfilled.

I had been involved in a number of home-based businesses through the years. From kitchen tools to candles to health and wellness, I dabbled in it all. I learned so much in each, but mainly it was self-development, reading to expand my knowledge base, learning to grow professionally, and learning how to dream big. It was the beginning of my believing I had more to offer the world.

Those businesses eventually fell by the wayside for one reason or another. I was tired of making only twenty percent of sales, compensation plan changes, and crazy high monthly autoships. If you have been in the direct selling and multi-level marketing arena, you know what I'm talking about.

In 2023, my dad began cancer treatment. After his final chemo, we were walking down the street of his little town that he had just moved to about a year prior. There was the cutest little building that was "for sale by owner," and it was the perfect size for a little gift shop. I had wanted a shop to call my own for years. Every time I found one, it was either too much money, had just entered into a contract, or was found after the fact. That afternoon, I called about it, my husband, dad, and I did a walk-through later that weekend, and not long after, the doors to our new gift shop were opened.

This began a seven-day work week. Monday-Friday were spent at my 9-5, then Friday evening until Sunday afternoon at the shop. I was doing the thing I had once prayed for. It was a lot, but I was beginning to live my dream, and I was thankful. That first season of being open was filled with learning, learning, and more learning! It was fun diving head-on into something that was completely new to us, but we jumped into it with blissful ignorance, pushing full steam ahead!

My dad was my biggest encourager, the one who lifted me up. He loved sitting in the rockers outside the shop, talking to customers and telling them to go in and check out the inside. He built shelves to hold products and would show up just to root me on, "check out the crowd," and tell me that I was going to have a great day. He was there when we did the ribbon cutting and took it upon himself to clean up around the shop when it needed it in the mornings before I opened. He moved more deliberately due to pain, but he wasn't going to miss out on anything that he could help with.

The cancer metastasized to his bones in a matter of months. He was in pain more often than not. I became his main caregiver, eventually staying with him seven days a week and working from his home. There was still a little time to go down to the shop on the weekends, though, because he would have it no other way. I also would have it no other way regarding his care. I always told him that I would be there to take care of him. Although it was the hardest thing I had done in my life, I was grateful to be with him during this time, lifting *him* now.

My priorities through this journey had shifted. The way my brain thought about life had transformed. I knew time was growing short. The cancer had diminished my strong, vibrant, and active dad into a twig of a man. It wasn't long until he passed away. My biggest encourager and my harshest critic was no longer here with me.

This year, we opened the shop for our third season. Part of me wanted to throw in the towel, sell it, rent it out, whatever. The grief made it hard to be there without him. I had to adjust, but I know he's with me in my heart, still cheering me on every day. When you lose someone you love so much, it can be hard to move forward, take the step, and start dreaming again. You want to give up and shrink into being a "regular, happy" person. You tell yourself that shrinking is okay, maybe this is your path. It's not.

A visit to my therapist brought it all back around and helped me immensely in reframing my thoughts and being able to move forward. I was long overdue for a tune-up and felt so much better walking out of that session. I am a huge advocate of mental health and regular therapy visits for the tune-ups. Consider them preventative maintenance for yourself!

Throughout taking care of my dad and after his passing, I came to the harsh realization that time waits for no one. I was reminded that I was made for such a time as this, and I have a God-given purpose in this world. I realized once again that I'm not satisfied with the status quo. I'll always want to be more, do more, and walk in my true self. For a while, and rightfully so, when caring for my dad, I had lost myself. I know he would not want me to stay that way. He was always pushing me to be better and not letting me feel down for too long.

You, too, have a God-given purpose in this world, right now! If you didn't, you would not be here right now, in this particular time in history. I encourage you to use your heartache as a propeller to lift you back up and to rise above the negative and allow yourself to dream again. What I've learned through my grief journey is that there are two versions of yourself. One that wants to settle into comfort and safety, staying the course and being consumed by the status quo. The other desires greatness, wants to feel strong and fearless, and continues growing and stretching beyond the self-imposed comfort zone.

Which are you? One of you has to go. Who will it be?

For a while, I was so consumed with grief that, if not for having to get up every morning for my job, I would have rotted in my bed. I was letting the old me, the one who craved comfort, take over. Make no mistake, I wasn't happy, but I wasn't ready to move forward. It was the "comfort zone" that I had lived in for the last 12 months, and I didn't want to dig myself out of the darkness, even though I knew I should. It wasn't until my therapy session that I was reminded of things: that I was so blessed to have a dad that loved me so much, that I was so blessed to have been able to care for him during his last months, that I was so blessed to hold his hand when he passed. I have no regrets. No words were left unsaid. It was time to take that step forward and start living again. Start dreaming again.

Are you going to let the old you win? Will you be satisfied if you do? I'm certainly not. When you are faced with death staring you straight in the face for months at a time, you look at life differently. You look at life in urgency, in "musts," in leaving it all on the table, and you have this increased desire to live your life, have new experiences, and create new memories. You let the things fall off that mean nothing anymore. Those things that used to bother you and get so easily under your skin? Those become nothing in life as they are no longer concerning to you because you're too busy living your life to the fullest, having the fun you've always wanted to, enjoying those around you, doing the things you've always wanted, and having no regrets. You're too busy dreaming again about life's possibilities. About lives you can impact. About the "legacy" or impression you will leave when it's your time to depart from this world. You can choose to dream or you can choose not to. The choice is completely yours.

For myself, I'm still busy with my 9-5, we still have the shop on the weekends, and I'm further moving into my true self. I've joined a new company that I align with, and I'm continuing to grow in my self-development. I also have a couple of other things I am currently working on. I'm living out my dream from years ago of being an author, right here and right now! I'm dreaming again and wanting to make the most of myself and my life…and doing those things I've always wanted to do so that when I'm on my deathbed, I can proudly say "I left it all on the table!"

If I can leave you with some words of encouragement, it would be to choose to dream. If it's your first time or you need a little push to begin doing so again, choose to dream! Dreaming helps open your mind to great possibilities in your life, gets you excited, and allows you to move toward a goal. Begin with a journal, writing down goals, what you're grateful for, and create a vision board. Don't go to bed tonight without putting a new (or old, dusty) dream into your mind. Dream big. Dream full. Dream in color. Knowing that you were made for more, made for a larger purpose. Put right where you are, in this time to do amazing things.

It all begins with you and a dream.

Patti Box is a creative entrepreneur, small business owner, and woman of faith committed to building a life of purpose and freedom. By day, she works in the corporate world, but she's steadily growing her gift shop and digital income stream, both born from her desire to create impact and live with intention. Patti finds joy in crafting, painting, cooking, and pursuing a healthy, holistic lifestyle. She's constantly learning and evolving, believing that each step taken in faith brings her closer to the life she's meant to live. Her contribution to this anthology is a reflection of her recent journey: a blend of courage, grit, and love. Patti believes life is too short not to chase your passions, even if it means taking small steps every day. She's honored to be part of a group of women encouraging one another and lifting each other up with strength and inspiration.

Please scan the QR code to connect with this author.

Linda Robinson

Knowledge Is Power: Pay It Forward

Because other women, from all social classes, chose to uplift and empower me, I became the leader I am today. Their support was not only powerful; it was transformational. They saw something in me before I fully saw it in myself. Their belief helped shape my path. Lack of confidence, impostor syndrome, and not knowing my value, I settled for a lot in my life and did not see myself as qualified for many roles during my corporate days. Because of so many women who have entered my life, they have helped me gain confidence, know my worth, and value myself. I am deserving of any and all roles that I feel are aligned with my passion and purpose in life.

During my time in corporate America, I had opportunities to be surrounded by women who saw the best in me. They made a way for me to grow and climb the corporate ladder. They provided me with training to enhance my leadership skills. It was during my time at A.G. Edwards and Wells Fargo that I saw many women from all backgrounds going back to school to continue to grow and develop in areas they were passionate about. Thank you to Meredith Goins-Anderson, Andrea Jackson, and so many other women for encouraging me to go back to school. This created opportunities to work on my degrees that will open doors.

In 2008, there was a merger that took place between Wachovia Securities and Wells Fargo. During this period, I met so many individuals who transferred to St. Louis after the merger, where I learned a valuable lesson that changed my life forever. I admired so many aspiring millennials. Jasmine Davis truly dropped some nuggets on me. Never stay in a position for more than three years. Take all the training you are offered and move on to the next. After three years, you have mastered the position, and you are no longer challenged. This has stuck with me as I move forward in my career.

At Webster University, through the Human Resource Development and Nonprofit Leadership program, I learned what it meant to lead with intention and authenticity. Under the guidance of some of my professors, I began to understand not just how to lead, but *why* we lead. We should lead with grace, confidence, and generosity. They opened doors I never expected to walk through, invited me into rooms where my voice was honored, and recognized me in spaces that gave me hope. They taught me how to be a fabulous woman and a fierce leader, and—most importantly—how to empower others in return. My professors are why I am the woman who has grown, stepped out of my comfort zone, and poured back into other women who are in the position I was in. This was a place of being scared and full of self-doubt. Those lessons stayed with me.

Later, at Big Brothers Big Sisters of Eastern Missouri, my first encounter with Ericka Sander was mind-blowing. She was the volunteer coordinator, but her knowledge, creative thinking, and passion were unforgettable. I saw a reflection of that same potential in Ericka that others had seen in me. I knew I had to lead and be her advocate to move her up at Big Brothers Big Sisters of Eastern Missouri. I saw greatness in her. Just like others did for me, I was able to offer Ericka hope, confidence, and the reassurance that she, too, belongs in every room she walks in. Being able to pour into her was one of the most meaningful full-circle moments of my leadership journey. Whatever opportunity or training she needed, I permitted her to take it. I was so excited when she told me she enrolled in school. Wow, she is on her way to being a true leader, to continue to be an advocate for the Big Brothers Big Sisters volunteer program.

When I gave my two weeks' notice, I told the leadership team that Ericka must be promoted to director of volunteer recruitment. She was the perfect candidate for that role. The knowledge, passion, creativity, innovative thinking, and relationships she had with the staff and Bigs are what was needed to move the organization forward. Yes, she was promoted!

Building confidence and empowering other women is more than a leadership principle—it is a calling. It is a gift from God. The ability to see someone's potential, speak life into their dreams, and help them step into their power is sacred work. It is not about authority or status; it is about service, trust, and love. Empowerment means reminding someone of who they are, especially when they have forgotten. It is helping a woman stand tall in rooms where she may have once shrank. It is saying, "You belong here"—and meaning it. When we empower others, we do not just give them strength to reflect it on themselves until they recognize it for themselves.

Mentorship is how that power grows and multiplies. It is how we pass the torch without losing our light. For women rising in their careers, mentorship can be the difference between hesitation and boldness, between feeling stuck and stepping forward. A mentor offers more than guidance—they offer perspective, lived experience, and encouragement at just the right moment.

As former First Lady Michelle Obama once said, *"When you have worked hard, and done well, and walked through that doorway of opportunity…You do not slam it shut behind you. You reach back and you give other folks the same chances that helped you succeed."*

I have been blessed by women who saw me, invested in me, and made space for me to lead. Now, I carry that forward—not out of obligation, but out of deep gratitude. Because every woman I mentor adds strength to a chain that stretches behind and ahead of me. Together, we climb. Together, we rise.

I am all about diversity, inclusion, and unity. This is why my network consists of women from all backgrounds, political views, religions, races, ethnicities, and the LGBTQIA community. As women, we must stay united, open doors for one another, offer a warm, welcoming space, and be one another's ally. It means a lot to me to support other women who do not look like me, be their voice, and stand with them. We all have a lot in common, more than we know.

As I reflect on my journey, my heart is filled with deep gratitude for the women who saw me before I fully saw myself. To every woman who spoke life into me, who opened a door, who offered a hand, who simply said, "You can"—thank you. You lifted me when I needed it most. You empowered me with your example and inspired me to become a woman of faith, purpose, and courage.

Because of other women, I have become a God-fearing leader who understands that strength does not mean doing it all alone. I have learned that my weaknesses are not flaws; they are opportunities for connection, humility, and growth. I now know that asking for help is not a sign of failure, but a sign of wisdom and trust in the people God has placed in my life.

We were never meant to climb alone. And I am so grateful I never had to.

Linda is an advisor-area director at ALSAC St. Jude, the fundraising and awareness organization for St. Jude Children's Research Hospital, with a Bachelor of Science in Communication, specializing in public relations from Lindenwood University, and two Master of Arts degrees, Human Resource Development and Nonprofit Management from Webster University. She co-founded the St. Louis Finest Volunteers team and earned numerous awards for its exceptional dedication to both nonprofit and for-profit organizations. Linda takes pride in her roles as a mother and grandmother and being a member of Friendly Temple Missionary Baptist Church. Linda's community and civic commitments include the Hatz 4 Hearts Foundation, Webster University's Alumni Association, St. Louis County Human Relations Commission, Maplewood Civil Service Commission, Board of Adjustment, and Housing Boards of Appeal. Linda is a passionate advocate for mental health, mental illness, and suicide prevention, serving as a family support group facilitator at NAMI STL and a volunteer with the American Foundation for Suicide Prevention.

Please scan the QR code to connect with this author.

Josephine Santana

We Heal. We Rise. We Build.

I've always had to be strong.

From a young age, I spent much of my free time working in my father's T-shirt printing shop, and through that experience, I learned hard work was non-negotiable. Complaints were met with more work, and tears were met with my parents asking, "You wanna cry? I'll give you something to cry about." Emotional intelligence wasn't prevalent in my home, and mental health was a taboo subject. In a typical Hispanic household, emotions aren't something you explore; they are something to be scolded for. You suck it up and keep moving.

Amidst the emotional warfare, I also learned early on that being quiet kept the peace. I wasn't the loud one. I often sat back, watching my sisters navigate the world while I stayed on the sidelines, observing, absorbing, and going through life quietly and alone. I didn't make waves. I didn't ask for help. I focused on keeping control to cope with the chaos, and when I joined the military, I carried that mindset with me.

In many ways, it helped me thrive. The discipline, structure, and clearly defined expectations gave me something solid to hold onto. As a young airman, I saw that many of the women in leadership shared the same mindset I had been raised with. They were tough. Stoic. Unshakable. They didn't show emotion, and if they struggled, you'd never know it. I admired them and assumed that's what I had to embody to succeed. So I modeled myself after them. I kept it together, never let anyone see me sweat, and did everything I could to prove I could handle the pressure just like they did.

As I grew into supervisory positions, I brought that same standard with me. I held myself to impossibly high standards and expected the same from my team. I pushed them to be sharp, composed, and high performing at all times, to which they delivered. They were promoted. They received recognition. They got the mission done.

I told myself I was doing it right; I was convinced that my leadership style was effective because we were "winning." What I didn't realize was that I wasn't leading them to thrive; I was teaching them how to survive just like I had.

In 2018, everything unraveled. The weight I'd been carrying, both professionally and personally, finally collapsed on me. I had spent years pretending to be fine—I had the uniform, the accomplishments, the results, but I was collapsing inside. When I finally needed help, I didn't know where to go. I was surrounded by people, but I didn't feel like I could be honest with anyone. I had built a reputation, but I hadn't built a support system. And in my darkest moments, I nearly died by suicide. I was breaking in plain sight, and no one knew.

That year forced me to stop, reflect, and confront myself. I had been carrying so much for so long that it became normal. When the pressure became too much, even for me, I had to ask why. That's when it hit me: I wasn't just carrying unrealistic expectations for myself; I had been placing those same expectations on my team. That realization hurt because I love my people. I believed I was pushing them to be great. I thought I was leading by example, but I had actually just passed down a version of strength that was rooted in silence, perfectionism, and emotional isolation. I had taught them how to survive without me, rather than thrive with me.

Yes, they were succeeding, but at what cost?

Were they carrying more than they should have just to keep up?

Were they pushing through things alone when they shouldn't have?

Although the truth was heavy, it was the catalyst for my personal and professional journey. I started to see leadership differently. It's not about driving people to perform; it's about creating space for them to grow. It's about helping them feel seen, not just evaluated. Supported, not just measured.

I also realized something else: *connection and community matter.*

The version of strength I had been taught, to stay quiet, figure it out alone, and not to burden others, almost broke me. I knew I wasn't the only one who had been operating that way, and I never want anyone under my leadership, a friend, or even a family member, to feel that isolated. So I made it my mission to build what I once needed. I started showing up differently. I listened more. I created space for conversations beyond just the task at hand. I encouraged my team to take care of themselves, to speak honestly, and to lead in a way that felt true to them. I even started showing up differently with my sisters. I chose vulnerability over silence and approached them with compassion, care, and understanding. It wasn't just about them understanding me; it was about me finally taking the time to understand them, too.

Then I began *building professional programs and platforms with intention.*

I now develop and lead leadership workshops focused on emotional intelligence and resilience because I believe those values are critical in fostering connection, compassion, and leaders who prioritize intention over ego. Building resilience isn't just about bouncing back; it's about equipping people with the tools to withstand pressure, navigate uncertainty, and continuously choose growth. Leadership is about more than checklists and outcomes; it's about who you are when things get hard and how you show up for others when they need you most.

I created Success Network Teams to help others set meaningful goals and support one another with shared purpose. These teams aren't just about accountability; they're about building community. Each member defines what success looks like for them, and together, we break those goals down into intentional, achievable steps. We celebrate progress, navigate setbacks, and lift each other up in the process. It's about creating a space where people feel seen, supported, and reminded that they don't have to chase growth alone.

I launched a resilience retreat for servicewomen and veterans as a space to pause, reflect, and reset without the pressure to perform or pretend everything's fine. It was intentionally designed as a judgment-free zone where women could take off the uniform, literally and figuratively, and focus on their own healing and growth. Through shared stories, meaningful connection, and intentional rest, the retreat became a place to breathe, be heard, and be reminded that strength also looks like stillness and vulnerability.

I offer mentorship to anyone who wants it, especially women in my career field, because if anyone gets it, it's me. Instead of expecting everyone to lead the way I once did, I meet people where they are to help them chase their own definition of success. I no longer believe in a one-size-fits-all approach. Authentic leadership means recognizing individual needs and providing personalized support to help people grow in their own direction.

One of the most important lessons I've learned is that ***vulnerability is not a weakness.***

That even senior leaders can take a knee.

That you can lead and still be human.

That you can be strong and still ask for help.

If I want to lift others, I must be willing to be seen, not just in strength, but in struggle too. That kind of leadership builds trust and changes lives.

Now, I tell people the things I wish someone had told me:

- You don't have to earn the right to struggle.

- You don't have to be perfect to be a good leader.

- You don't have to carry it all alone.

I come from a place of survival, but I lead from a place of purpose. The legacy I want to leave isn't about how far I've climbed; it's about how many people I've helped rise along the way. ***Together, we heal. We rise. We build.***

Josephine "Josie" Santana is a second-generation mixed Latina from West Chicago with over 21 years of service in the United States Air Force. Determined to create a brighter future, she turned early life challenges into motivation, finding purpose and structure through military service. She holds a bachelor's degree in human resource management and is currently pursuing a graduate degree in industrial/organizational psychology.

Josie is a certified Department of the Air Force leadership coach and a John C. Maxwell team member. She has facilitated several leadership and professional development seminars, investing hundreds of hours into mentorship to help others grow with purpose, resilience, and confidence. Known for creating emotionally intelligent and inclusive spaces, Josie leads with heart and authenticity, ensuring others feel seen, valued, and supported as they navigate their own leadership journey.

Her impact has earned her multiple accolades, including the Military Outstanding Volunteer Service Medal and the Air Force Materiel Command Wilma Vaught Innovative Leadership Award. Her journey is a testament to grit, heart, and the belief that lifting others is the highest form of leadership.

Please scan the QR code to connect with this author.

Annetta Works Salley

Legacy: Honoring the Power of the Sister Circle Lineage

"We are surrounded by a great cloud of witnesses..."
—Hebrews 12:1

Before I ever spoke my first word or took my first breath, a circle of women had already surrounded me with prayers, purpose, and power. I call them my *Daughters of Pearl*. This is a lineage woven from faith, fire, and fierce love. These were not just women; they were watchwomen of my soul, including my great-grandmother Alberta, my grandmother Pearl, and my mother Pearl. Each one held a corner of the mantle that would eventually fall on me. Their voices echo in my spirit, their wisdom dances in my decisions, and their strength sustains me. You see, a Sister Circle is not a moment—it's a movement. It is a divine formation of women bonded by love, forged through shared experience, and committed to seeing one another rise. A Sister Circle Lineage is something even deeper that transcends time and bloodlines. It connects ancestors to descendants through the work of legacy. The women in my lineage didn't just love me; they prepared me.

This is not just my story. It is our story. It is the unfolding of a sacred trust passed from one generation to the next. And now, it is my turn to carry it forward, not only in memory, but in mission. This is the power of the Sister Circle Lineage.

My First Sister Circle: Daughters of Pearl

My first Sister Circle was made up of the women who literally and spiritually carried me into being: my Great Grandma Alberta, Grandma Pearl, and Mama Pearl. These three wise women covered me in prayer consistently, faithfully, and purposefully. Their collective years of living held enough experience, joy, wisdom, and truth to fill volumes. That wisdom was passed on to me through storytelling and spirit-nurturing, cultivating my space to live my "beautiful" authentically, intentionally, and unapologetically. These women didn't just raise me, they formed me. And I am connected to this Sister Circle not only by blood, but by divine assignment. My story is a continuation of their prayers, dreams, and sacrifices. It's a divine plan filled with a future that will not be complete until I meet my Creator. The values cultivated in this circle were faith, family, and security. These were the arms that rocked me, the hands that held mine, and the shoulders that carried me until I could stand tall enough to lift others.

My Grandma Pearl was a quiet force of nature. In her mid-fifties, she returned to school to be certified as a dietitian cook, proving that it is never too late to invest in your calling. Make no mistake, she already had decades of experience feeding the body and soul. Grandma Pearl was no stranger to cooking for over 200 people, children and staff alike, every single day. For her, cooking wasn't a job. It was an art.

She passed that art down to my Mama Pearl, who took it and stirred in her own spice. Watching the two of them in a kitchen was like watching a symphony of grace and grit. The way they moved, measured, tasted, laughed, and loved was something sacred. You didn't just eat their food: you experienced it. It looked good, smelled heavenly, tasted divine, and, most importantly, it made you feel seen. Long before it became a trendy phrase, Grandma and Mama knew the power of "holding space for a sister." Whether you were heartbroken or hungry, confused or celebrating, their kitchen was a sanctuary. It was therapy without judgment, prayer without preaching, nourishment beyond the plate.

Let's talk about the dinner table, because in our house, eating together was not optional. No TV. No phone. No wandering away from the table early. When Mama said dinner would be ready in thirty minutes, she meant thirty. Not twenty-nine. Not twenty-five. Thirty. If the phone rang during dinner, whew, help us, Lord! Whoever dared to call more than once might get a holy earful. I didn't fully understand it then, but I sure do now. They were protecting something sacred: time, presence, and connection.

From that table, I walked away with golden rules that continue to guide me:

1. Treat others how you deserve to be treated, that it may be well with your soul.

2. Set boundaries and communicate them clearly, so others know how to engage with you.

3. Say what you mean and mean what you say, in all conversations.

Simple? Maybe, but in a world full of noise, those rules became anchors.

Even now, when I set a table, light a candle, or cook with intention, I feel them with me. Their spirits guide my hands. Their words remind me of my worth. Their strength tells me that my legacy didn't begin with me, and it certainly doesn't end with me.

My Second Sister Circle: The Aunties

My second Sister Circle, the Aunties, was a sanctuary of support and encouragement. Made up of Great Aunt Bertha, Aunt Billie Sue, and Aunt

Janet, this circle taught me that sometimes the most powerful act of love is helping someone find their voice. Who doesn't need encouragement and support? This circle was filled with love and a sincere desire to nurture my potential through unwavering faith in God, celebrating life without apology, and practicing social justice in everyday opportunities.

My Aunt Janet once told me, "Your story is for helping change narratives and build bridges." That wisdom gave me permission to show up in rooms where I once felt invisible. They reminded me that confidence is built through public speaking and that no one should speak for you when God has given you something to say. They taught me to take time to laugh, dance, and celebrate with the ones who love my "beautiful" and to never apologize for doing so.

The values cultivated in this Sister Circle were authentic relationships, living in purpose, and curiosity. This was all fuel for a life of fearless becoming.

My Third Sister Circle: The Sisters

My third Sister Circle is made up of my sisters, Christine and Denise. They are the ones who have witnessed my journey in real time. With them, I moved from being the one nurtured to becoming a nurturer myself. Our sisterhood is where iron sharpens iron. We have cried together, prayed together, laughed until we couldn't breathe, and called each other higher even when it was uncomfortable.

Unlike the generations before us, our relationship required navigating new terrain, blending tradition with transformation, reverence with rawness. Christine teaches me about stillness and strength; Denise teaches me about fire and faith. Together, they help me remain grounded and growing. In them, I see the continuation of the legacy. The baton was passed not just in name, but in calling.

The lesson learned from this circle is that sisterhood is not just what you receive, it's what you give back. It is about showing up whole and honest, even when you're healing. With Christine and Denise, I have learned the power of truth-telling, the gift of presence, and the beauty of becoming.

The values cultivated here are transparency, loyalty, and shared responsibility for the legacy we carry forward. This Sister Circle doesn't just surround me; it walks beside me. Through it, I learned that legacy is not something we simply inherit. It is something we choose to live. This realization, this shift from receiving to stewarding, became the turning point. It's my awakening.

Annetta Works Salley is a speaker, storyteller, and purpose cultivator who believes in the transformative power of legacy, sisterhood, and sacred presence. She draws from her lineage of strong women to inspire others to rise, reflect, and lead with intention.

Annetta is the founder of *iCelebrateU365*, a personal ministry and reflective blog dedicated to honoring everyday victories and cultivating safe spaces for intergenerational conversations and creative expressions that spark positive change—one story, one voice, one heart at a time.

Her debut contribution to a published anthology, *Legacy: Honoring the Power of the Sister Circle Lineage*, is both a milestone and a mission, an offering of gratitude to the women who shaped her and a call to action for those she's called to reach.

Annetta resides in Southwestern Illinois with her husband and beloved furbaby, continuing to hold space for women to grow, heal, and become—boldly and beautifully.

Please scan the QR code to connect with this author.

Luisa Otero Prada

The Unknown

I once heard that starting something means you've already completed fifty percent of the task. That feels true in my case. I think deeply before beginning anything. I play it out in my mind first, envisioning the details, foreseeing possible challenges, and working through potential solutions. Whether it's a painting, an art project, or a proposal, I often feel like I've already made significant progress by the time I begin. This gives me a sense of confidence and momentum, but something unexpected almost always happens. A surprising element appears, either magical or disappointing. That is ***the unknown.***

"Do you fear the unknown?" the doctor asked me while examining my five-month-old son, Nicolás. My instinct was to say "yes," but instead, we—my son's father, my mother, the doctor's assistant, and I—started a conversation about what the unknown really is.

We think we know, but we don't. We don't know what tomorrow holds. We base our ideas on yesterday or today, but life continually exposes us to the unknown. It can be frightening, or it can be beautiful.

Who was I, at that moment in the doctor's office? I was a woman who grew up in the Atlantic region of Colombia, in a small city by the Sinú River and just two hours from the Caribbean Sea. A place where life used to slow down between noon and 2 p.m., when everyone heads home for lunch and a siesta, or simply to lie down and watch the ceiling fan spin away the heat.

I grew up in a beautiful, nurturing family. My parents, both educated and progressive, raised us with open minds and strong values. They both attended Catholic boarding schools. My mother once dreamed of becoming a missionary nun—an unusual one, who would live among indigenous communities, learning from them, connecting with their relationship to nature, and admiring their crafts. Though romantic in her vision, she was also aware of the sacrifices and spiritual commitments her path would have required. "Mystic" is the word that best describes my mother.

My father, an architect, was full of charisma and vision—100% a dreamer and doer. A mystic and a visionary raised four children in a Caribbean city far from their own hometowns but full of hope and ambition. Our home was filled with books about different cultures, religions, and ways of life. I remember when my father bought us a full encyclopedia set. This was a joyful day! Friends came over often to do homework. I played chess with my father, who taught me patiently. I painted beside my mother from a very young age. I loved accompanying my father to visit the construction sites of the homes he was building. As the oldest daughter, the *primogénita*, I felt a strong sense of responsibility. I enjoyed it. I was happy, but then, there was *the unknown*.

I don't remember exactly when I realized I had an asymmetrical smile, a facial paralysis. Maybe around second grade, when some classmates pointed it out and teased me. A few gave me cruel nicknames. Even my younger sister—outgoing and brave—would defend me when she saw someone being unkind. My parents took me to see doctors in other cities. They wanted to help me in any way they could. They eventually took me to Dr. Salomón Hakim in Bogotá. He was a gentle, brilliant neurosurgeon who exuded wisdom. He examined my five-year-old face and then told my mother, "Don't let anyone touch your daughter's face. Science isn't ready to help her surgically; maybe when she's 18 or 20." He encouraged me to play the flute, to whistle, and to do a mirror exercise every day: wink my right eye 100 times or more.

After that visit, the medical appointments ended, and the mirror became a constant in my life. Every day I tried to do my exercises.

I was a good student who loved school. My notebooks were colorful and full of drawings. I remember a teacher asking for my Spanish notebook, and I felt obligated to give it to her. That happened often. I gave away many of my beautiful notebooks to teachers and friends, full of illustrated maps, and book reports with watercolor scenes. At home, my daily mirror work became the requirement to access anything else I wanted. If I wanted dance classes, I had to promise to do my facial exercises first. The flute and whistle never stuck because I wasn't musically inclined. I had a loving home, but every day I was reminded that I needed to "fix" something about myself.

On the outside, people saw me as talented, intelligent, and responsible. On the inside, I began to feel imperfect. I wasn't "beautiful enough." I felt pressure to compensate for that by being exceptional at everything else. I liked being seen as intelligent, but over time, it became a burden. I was just a little girl, eight, nine, ten years old, carrying the weight of trying to be perfect.

At some point, my mother started exploring alternative treatments for my face. By then, we had moved to a larger city with more cultural opportunities. My sister joined a dance academy, and I went to my aunt's children's art school, "*Miguel Ángel*." My aunt, a graduate of the *Bellas Artes* school, was a pioneer in children's art. Her academy was magical, filled with kids like me. I loved painting suns and skies. In three public murals commissioned by the mayor's office, I was responsible for painting those elements. I never imagined I'd paint murals again later in life. Art academy, swimming, and athletics filled my days at twelve. I even trained for hurdles and showed promise, but I had to quit to begin acupuncture therapy. My mother and I went to see this doctor every week for over a year. While I appreciated her efforts and felt hopeful, the results were minimal.

Eventually, we moved back to our hometown. I resumed school in eighth grade at a Catholic co-ed school. I thrived at this school, and I loved it. I made lifelong friends. By the time I graduated, I had decided to stop focusing on my facial paralysis. In Bogotá, the colder climate seemed to relax my facial muscles a bit. My friends said it was less noticeable. I didn't seek acupuncture again. Instead, I discovered meditation and breathing, alongside beer, music, friendships, and love.

At sixteen, I started university to study architecture just like my father. I was creative and hardworking. One of my professors told me, "You have what it takes to be a great architect." Sometimes, my colorful and expressive project presentations intimidated others. Some wondered why I wasn't in the art faculty, but I was determined to be an architect. In my final year, I was selected to represent my university at a national architecture competition of seventeen faculties, and I placed second. I should have been proud, but I felt disappointed. I let that moment discourage me. I now know I should've celebrated it. It was a milestone, not a failure.

I practiced architecture, and I fell in love. A year later, we were married. After six years of ups and downs, I became pregnant with Nicolás. He was a beautiful baby with golden hair, and I was ready. I had helped raise my younger brother. I read every book and thought I was prepared. Nicolás cried constantly. Breastfeeding was difficult. He barely slept. We saw all the best pediatricians in our city, and then in others. Nothing helped. Months passed. He slept maybe three hours a day. Then came the doctor who asked, "Do you fear the unknown?"

He examined Nicolás with magnifiers and strange, polished needles. That night, my son slept longer than ever before. I didn't care what method the doctor had used; he had helped my child. We continued seeing him for a year. He finally told us, "I've done all I can. Nicolás is a different child now. It's time for specialists, therapies, and strategies." This began our true journey into the unknown.

We began taking Nico to neurologists, requesting tests for his brain, vision, and hearing. The results were inconclusive—he was "borderline," a word that offered no clarity. No one could tell us if he'd walk, read, or what to expect. Looking for more, we found The Institutes for the Achievement of Human Potential in Pennsylvania. Their book, *What to Do About Your Brain-Injured Child,* gave us hope. His father and I took their week-long course, which became a turning point. Back in Bogotá, we joined *Taller Huellas*, an early stimulation center. I shared what we had learned and spent every day with Nico from 8 a.m. to 5 p.m. At age three, after a year, Nico began walking. He loved balloons, so I used them to motivate him, first on flat ground, then on grass to challenge his balance. His gait was wide and unsteady, but he always stayed on his feet.

Eventually, we moved to the U.S. seeking more support and guidance. Though we still lacked a firm diagnosis, we focused on supporting the brain, not chasing labels. That mindset became our guide. Moving to the U.S. was never a dream of mine. I didn't have the "American Dream." I just wanted to do whatever I had to do for my son. Fortunately, Nico's father had U.S. residency, and it was possible to bring us here.

This was a new country with a new language. It was a completely different life, but some things stayed the same, like doctors, therapies, and specialists. It was a relief that everyone we met seemed genuinely interested in helping Nico. I spent most of my days driving from appointment to appointment, and I felt a renewed sense of hope.

Then it was time for a special preschool. Nico's classroom was filled with incredible people, including his teacher, Diane, and his one-on-one aide, Barb. They didn't just help Nico. They helped me too, lifting me up. Every time, they told me my English was beautiful. I was trying. I joined ESL classes at the library, and I found a wonderful tutor, a father of a 31-year-old son with special needs. Our conversations were mostly about our children. Despite the age difference, we shared so much. Later, I found a quote from the Baha'i faith that reminded me of all the kind people who had crossed our path:

"Do not be content with showing friendship in words alone, let your heart burn with loving kindness for all who may cross your path."
Baha'u'llah

There are so many stories from this life with my son. The most important one is that Nico is here to teach me, every single day. He teaches me patience, humility, and perseverance, and he gives me the most incredible hugs and smiles. Life kept evolving. I got divorced, moved from New Jersey to St. Louis, and, in love again, remarried a very kind man. I became a wife, a stepmother, and gained a beautiful new family. You can imagine the joyful and complicated stories. What matters most is that Nico is deeply loved and continues to bring love wherever he goes. My family, my mother, father, siblings, in-laws, nieces, nephews, aunts, uncles, cousins, and Nico's family from his father's side have been there for us. Over the past 21 years in St. Louis, we've built a new family, one that walks beside us. I've also not had many friends, but just enough. All you need is good friends. I am grateful every day for my few extraordinary *amigas*.

Today, my son is 27. He is a gentle soul with blue eyes and an unforgettable smile. He has multiple diagnoses: a neurogenetic condition called Angelman syndrome, mild to moderate autism, visual impairment, sensory processing disorder, and he is nonverbal. He walks, he runs, he is a pal, and he radiates joy. I don't know exactly where in my path I made the decision to enjoy my son the way he was, and I decided my son wasn't a tragedy. If he wasn't going to college, it was completely fine. But I did...I made that decision. I wanted to have fun with Nico, enjoying his silliness, his rocking body, and flappy hands, and supporting him with grace and joy, giving thanks every day for his presence in my life.

I've learned:

Lives don't need to be fixed. They need to be supported. Children—and adults—with diverse needs, different abilities, and neurodiverse minds are not here to be changed. They're here to help us become better human beings. They teach us unconditional love, and they lift us up. They teach us how to embrace *the unknown.*

Luisa Otero Prada is a Colombian-born American visual artist based in St. Louis since 2004. She has an architecture degree from La Salle University in Bogotá. Her vibrant, expressive paintings are rooted in colors, flora, and people exploring identity and connection.

Luisa is active in St. Louis' arts scene. She completed programs with the Regional Arts Commission, held residencies through Artscope and the Contemporary Art Museum, and led workshops, public art, and curatorial projects with local organizations.

Her work has been exhibited in nearly 60 shows across four states and featured in the Missouri History Museum's Emerging Immigrant Artist showcase.

Luisa was a 2022–2023 Emerging Artist at the St. Louis Art Fair, a Mid-America Arts Alliance Artist Leadership Fellow, and an Artist INC facilitator. Since 2021, she has served as youth programs coordinator for Bread and Roses Missouri and was honored with the 2024 Visionary Award for Community Impact Artist.

Please scan the QR code to connect with this author.

Jaclyn Noroño-Rodriguez

Pillars and Lessons Are All Around You

Building your character can be compared to building a house. You start from nothing, and slowly you create the structure and everything inside of it. You can only do so much on your own. Eventually, you have to accept that you need help. You reach out to subject matter experts, you get advice, you change things, and you keep growing. Sometimes things break, sometimes nature hits, sometimes all things happen, just like throughout life. Just like in life, even with the tumbles, you somehow manage to remodel, rebuild, and stay standing thanks to your foundation and your pillars.

I have been blessed with very strong pillars throughout my life, both men and women who have lifted me up. There are so many wonderful ladies in my life that I would need multiple books to highlight them all. Every woman in my life has been a pillar, and they all have taught me many lessons. I'd like to share seven lessons from my core pillar group and the qualities I added to my own house (character) as a result.

Reach the Unthinkable

My mom led by example in terms of strength. All throughout my life, she has been fierce, strong, and independent. As I looked around, not only within my broader family, but also my friends' moms, my mom simply stood out as she was the professional career woman. I was (and still am) so proud to be her daughter. Even though she worked many hours, she always made time for us. As I grew older, I realized how different a world my mom grew up in versus the world I grew up in. Women were not engineers back in the day; women were not professionals or career-minded, and yet she broke the mold and stepped out into the world. The more I learn about my mom's life, the more I am in awe of everything she has accomplished. That's how I started crafting who I wanted to be. I wanted to reach the unthinkable just like her, who lifted others up.

Be Kind No Matter What

I met "K" in college, quickly learning of her Christian devotion, which eventually found its way into my heart and spirit. She was a ball of joy all the time, and I grew continuously amazed at her demeanor and her way of life. What struck me the most about her was how she was kind to everyone around her and always thought of others before herself. She is the one who would buy an extra meal and give it to the unhoused when given the opportunity. I will admit I was not as selfless or kind as she was, but her continuous influence changed me. She taught me that kindness always prevails, which does not mean life will not throw you tough curveballs; it just means that being kind will take you further. Regardless of the tough times, she remained focused on doing good for others. She has been there for me in the good, the bad, and the ugly. God guided her into my life, and eventually I found God myself. Then, I added kindness and selflessness to my own house and character.

Stay Active While You Can

I immigrated to the United States when I was sixteen years old to start college. As part of my culture immersion experience, I started working at Mamma-E's Italian-Latin restaurant. I was blown away by how she approached life. Not only was she a warrior professional owning her own business, but she was the one cooking at her home, doing the finances of her business, and still being the mom in a family of five. She is the one who organized all weekend activities and made sure they always involved outdoor activities. I know for a fact she walks at least 2-5 miles every day. To this day, we have a running joke with her telling us "Let's go for a super quick walk" and ending up walking 10 miles or more. Needless to say, we don't believe her "quick walks" anymore! She was (and still is) as active as ever, leading by example. With this, I added vigorous to my character-aspired qualities, because of her.

Family and Friends' Togetherness is Priority

They say that the apple doesn't fall far from the tree, and I really do see why. As I became part of Mamma-E's circle of friends and family, I met her oldest daughter. I'd love to pinpoint the exact moment within the last 25 years that my friendship with her turned to sisterhood, but I really can't. It just happened. Watching her through time turn into the kick-butt, outstanding entrepreneur mom she is today has been a blessing. But what continues to amaze me is her innate ability to bring people together, how much she does for others, and how welcoming she is to those around her. Everyone who meets her loves her instantly. She always made it a priority to have "family and friends" time, and through the years, they all adopted me as part of their family. I then got to be a continuous part of the amazing togetherness that it brought on. I distinctly remember the day she met my now-husband and how she immediately made him feel part of us. He has shared with me how much he treasured not only the welcome but the continuous connection she created. Her kiddos, "C" and "S," are, for all intents and purposes, my niece and nephew, and I love them with all my heart. They are such wonderful human beings and always close to family and friends, proving once again that the apple does not fall far from the tree. Thanks to her, I added "family/friends focus" to my pillar of aspired qualities.

Puzzle Pieces Support Each Other

I am blessed to have a group of superwoman friends, and we call ourselves the puzzle pieces. It all started with necklaces of puzzle pieces that together made up a heart that I got us all a few Christmases ago. The idea behind it was that we are puzzle pieces in each other's lives, and it just stuck! These women have taught me so much. They have been with me through the ups and downs of life for a little over twelve years. We are there for each other to vent, to cry, to laugh, to watch TikTok videos and reels (the new way of communicating), and all throughout life's rollercoasters. The biggest lesson, though, that I'm still learning, is that it's ok to be vulnerable, to need support, and then to be humble enough to accept it. I realize it's not common to have this type of friendship, to have women with whom you can really be yourself—100 percent. I treasure my dear puzzles wholeheartedly and thus added "vulnerable" to my pillar of aspired qualities.

Above Anything, Be Human

Throughout my career, I have been blessed to have some pretty amazing women who stepped into my life and made a difference, lifting others up. When Mrs. "S" came to be my direct supervisor, my professional world changed forever. The biggest lesson she has taught me, and candidly, continues to teach me, is that it's ok to be human. Her ability to lead, to support, to coach, to be tough yet gentle, to be so down to earth (which makes me want to go above and beyond all the time) is astounding! An example of this was when I was going through some very difficult personal times, and her immediate response was "Take whatever time you need to heal." In the midst of everything I was dealing with, those words and her unwavering support gave me peace within the storm. I was able to take the time to heal without having to worry about my professional role suffering. That's when it hit me: life happens to everyone, and we are all human. That is exactly the type of leader and pillar I aspire to be. One who is human, who understands when life happens, and shows grace to those around me. And thus I added "humaneness" to my pillar of aspired qualities.

Spread the Gift of Faith

My mother-in-law lives in Costa Rica, and she became a mom while she was very young. She raised three wonderful men, one of them being my hubby, and she raised them with God all throughout. The values that I most admire about my husband undoubtedly come from her. I still remember one of the first few times my husband (then boyfriend) and I were at church together, and he was singing all the hymns by heart! When I asked him about it, he mentioned his mom would take them to church to learn about God. Truth is, I see her in him all throughout daily interactions as he keeps God as a priority in our lives, displaying strong family and personal values. This can be observed even in how he manages difficult situations, keeping faith alive even when it's hard to. I can only hope that when I get the blessing to be a mother, I get the chance to follow my mother-in-law's example and raise a woman or man of God. I hope to be a pillar of faith for my future children.

All in all, the people in my life, along with my experiences, have shaped who I am today. I simply would not be here without them, and I take it to heart to pay it forward to the men and women around me and as part of my legacy to my future children. Reach the unthinkable, be kind no matter what, keep family and friends as priority, be human, and spread faith all around you, and your house will turn out to be the strongest for sure.

Please be very selective about who you surround yourself with; let those around you be people who inspire you, support you, and look to be a positive part of your life. Bring together the right set of "expertise" for your home, look for those who are where you want to be, those who will help when help may be needed. Pay attention first to those who show up during the tough times when nature hits, and the ones who also make time to celebrate the good times. My mom used to always say, *"Dime con quien andas y te dire quien eres,"* which means "Tell me who you hang out with, and I'll tell you who you are." She was completely right. So my message to you is to choose your pillars wisely. They will shape you by instilling in you good habits that will undoubtedly lead to good results. Your pillars will hold you when life hits you, and you will persevere through storms thanks to them. Build yourself a strong house (character) as you strengthen your forever home (self).

Lastly, do not forget to pay it forward when given the chance to lift others up. Whether you know it or not, you are likely a pillar for someone around you, so stand tall and be your best version of you. I have been surprised when key women around me tell me things like "I am inspired by you," "I admire you," and "You have made a difference in my life." It was an "aha" moment for me; turns out everyone around you is watching you, and they are also learning from you. When friends come to you for advice, that means they rely on you to help them with whatever the challenge is. Try your best to be there for them in the good and the not-so-great times. That means you are their pillar. Be the strongest pillar and rely on your pillars to withstand whatever nature throws at you. You got this.

A native Venezuelan, Jaclyn came to the United States on a college scholarship. She lives in Missouri with her *Tico* husband, Carlos. After graduating from high school from Apamates (Maracaibo), she earned a BS in business management systems from Drury University, an MBA from Webster University, and a leadership certificate from the Hispanic Leadership Institute (*Clase* VIII!).

Her career has taken her across industries, including food and beverage, financial institutions, manufacturing, and operations. She is currently the director of business development for Packaging Solutions at DHL Supply Chain and sits on the board of directors for the Venezuelan Association in Missouri.

When asked about her major achievements, she proudly shared how, with her husband's help, they purchased a home for her parents and brother who lived in Venezuela. They moved in last year, and the family is back together after being apart for 23 years! The next step is to grow the family.

Please scan the QR code to connect with this author.

Catalina Valdez

The Fight: For Resilience and Tradition

I don't have fancy words. I only have my truth, and it begins with love—love for my traditions, my roots, and everything my family taught me. That love has guided me in this journey of protecting and sharing *el buen comer*, the art of good, conscious eating through our traditional foods.

In today's world, with everything so fast, processed, and industrialized, it's hard to keep our old ways alive. But I believe our food carries our history. Our ingredients carry our identity. When we prepare meals the way our mothers and grandmothers once did, we are not just feeding our stomachs, we are feeding our spirits and remembering who we are.

Traditional food tells a story. It reminds us of home. It reminds us of sitting at the table with our mother's warmth in every bite. It brings back memories of a grandmother who knew exactly what broth to make when we had a stomachache. These meals were medicine. They were love.

I came to the United States in 1996. I arrived in the suburbs northeast of Chicago, alone, with many limitations. I was a Mexican woman, undocumented, didn't speak English, and didn't know what the future held. But like many immigrants, I came with the dream of helping my family back in Oaxaca. That dream gave me strength.

I started working in restaurants, doing whatever job I could get. At one point, I even dressed in a monkey costume to promote pizza. Over time, I worked my way up to manager. In 23 years, I did almost every job you can do in a restaurant. I worked hard because I needed to send money home.

But something never sat right with me. The food I served wasn't like the food I grew up with. It was fast, it was processed, and it didn't nourish people. I missed the flavors of my mother's kitchen—the *adobos*, the *moles*, the fresh vegetables, but I had no time to cook. I worked 17 hours a day. Time, like health, had become a luxury.

That's when I stopped eating meat and became a vegetarian. Not because I wanted to follow a trend, but because I couldn't prepare food the way I believed it should be. For many years, I didn't eat traditional Mexican food because I couldn't make it the right way.

In the middle of working, surviving, and chasing dollars, life brought deep pain. I lost a child during pregnancy. Later, I separated from my husband. Then, I lost my mother. One day, in 2009, after my divorce, I found myself at a library, trying to make sense of my life. I started reading books about self-improvement, and that's when I found *Rich Dad, Poor Dad*. That book opened my eyes and planted a seed: maybe I could have a business. Maybe my dream could live.

My biggest dream was to open a small restaurant. Even just three tables would be enough, if it meant I could share Oaxacan food with others, the way my mother used to cook. She used to make *caldos*, little broths with chopped vegetables, simple and healing. She called them *calditos nacos*, not to shame them, but because they were humble. She cooked with love and from what the earth gave us.

But starting a restaurant here in the U.S. felt like a distant dream. I didn't speak English well. I still struggle with it. I try, but something happened when I was young that made it harder. When I was 15, I was in a coma for three months. I didn't realize how much that would affect me later in life. Still, I never focused on what I couldn't do. I kept going.

At work, people laughed at me. They said I was crazy for dreaming. I used to go to business seminars after my shifts. They'd say, "Look at her, dreaming with her eyes open." It hurt, but I kept learning. In 2014, I paused my food business idea and started working as a distributor of health supplements. Even in that space, my heart stayed with health and wellness.

Distributing supplements taught me how to talk to people and how to handle rejection. I traveled to different states in the U.S. to meet customers and attend trainings. One phrase from those trainings stayed with me: "*El deseo ardiente*"—the burning desire to make your dreams real. That phrase gave me hope.

After five years of hard work, I had saved some money. In May 2019, I traveled to St. Louis. My nephew had told me about a restaurant for sale. The name of the restaurant was *Lucha*, which means "fight." That word described my life perfectly.

I met with the owner and, without much thinking, I said yes. We closed the deal quickly. But I didn't know what I was getting into. I had worked in restaurants for decades, but I had never owned one. After the pandemic hit, the restaurant needed a lot of changes, and I wasn't ready.

When my business partner left, I had to figure everything out alone. We didn't have systems in place. Everything fell on me. It was overwhelming. I cried many nights. All of our 21 employees left. It was just me, my husband Mario, and my niece Francia. The three of us kept *Lucha* alive.

I had to learn how to use a computer. In school, I had never even used a calculator. It was hard. But little by little, I learned. A friend, Ricardo Martínez, came to help me with marketing. I watched him closely and learned everything I could. Eventually, I started doing all the administrative work on my own.

I am so grateful to the people who stood by me during that time: my husband Mario, my sister Ana, and my accountant and dear friend Mike Jones. They believed in me when others didn't.

In June 2023, while participating in Carlo Márquez's *Fundadores* program, something new was born: *Lucha Oaxaca Savory*. I created two products—*mole* and *adobo*. My goal was to offer something 100% natural that honored our traditions and gave people back two important luxuries: health and time.

To build the brand and open *A. Careva Corp.*, I once again relied on the support of Mario and Mike. I will never forget their loyalty.

At the restaurant, I always told my team: Dream big. Work for your goals. One of my employees, Rafael, listened. He worked hard and eventually started his own brand of gym supplements. That made me proud. I helped him rise.

Now, when I look back, I understand that you don't have to be the strongest or the fastest. What matters is that you keep going. That you don't give up. If you have a dream in your heart, take the first step. Don't wait. Don't let excuses like age, status, or fear keep you from moving forward. If you don't act, your dream might stay buried forever.

Through food, especially food made with intention, I encourage women to rise and take care of their health and well-being. We only get one body in this life. We must care for it. I find joy in feeding others. When I feel like giving up, I remember the words of my mother.

She couldn't read or write, but she had so much wisdom:

"Estudia mijita para que seas una gran injeniera y tengas mucho dinero."
"Study, *mijita*, so you can be a great engineer and have money."

"Las mujeres podemos con eso y más."
"We women can handle this and more."

"Las mujeres somos chingonas."
"Women are 'tough.'"

"Mellito asi como eres retobona conmigo debes ser con los problemas y que nadie te pare"
"*Mellito*, just like you're stubborn with me, be that way with your problems; don't let anything stop you."

"No que muy chingosita"
"Weren't you tough? Prove it."

And I do. Every day, I try.

Xcanadi xquiiñe gaca guidxi layu.
Seguimos en la lucha por la tradición.

Catalina Valdez was born in Tlacolula de Matamoros, Oaxaca. She began cooking at the age of six out of necessity, and today she sees it as her duty to preserve her roots and teach future generations the value of tradition. She is a fashion designer, chef, owner of *Lucha Restaurant* in St. Louis, and founder of *Lucha Oaxaca Savory*, a brand of natural, traditional Oaxacan foods. Catalina has worked as a distributor for Omnilife for 28 years and is a proud member of the Hispanic Chamber of Commerce in the St. Louis Metro area. She believes that through food, we can heal, connect, and remember who we are.

Please scan the QR code to connect with this author.

Anita Hansen

Tamales, Meatballs, and Hot Dogs

Who am I? I am a "Mexi-Swede-American." What is that, you ask? That is the good-ole fashion American dream of two immigrants from two countries separated by oceans who immigrated to the USA to build a better future. Along their journey, they met in an airport, fell in love, got married, and about a year later…well, that's where I come into the picture and where my story begins.

My mother is a *Mexicana* and my father is Swedish. I'm a first-generation American. You don't find too many "Mexi-swedes" or "swex-i-cans." Growing up in a household where multiple languages and cultures came together was a lot of fun, but sometimes confusing. Many of my Mexican American friends and family on my mom's side spoke "Spanglish," but English was the dominant language in our house. My mother couldn't speak Swedish, and my dad only knew a little Spanish, which was mostly slang and curse words. Although I never became fully fluent in Spanish or Swedish, I learned to swear in three languages.

This was the same with my grandparents. My *abuelo* and *abuela* spoke only Spanish. My dad's parents mainly spoke Swedish, but *Farfar* (Swedish for "grandpa") practiced his English every time they came to visit. They also *loved* my mom's cooking. Tacos are very popular in Sweden, and they even have a night dedicated to eating Mexican food, called "Taco Fridays," which is like our American norm of "Taco Tuesday."

I was one of a kind (well, two of a kind if you include my little sister) who didn't know any different than her current comfortable world. I was born in South Texas and moved up to St. Louis at a very young age with my older half-siblings when my dad got a job at TWA Airlines. My little sister, Annie, was born two years later when we were already settled in Missouri. My normal was much different than my school and neighborhood friends in St. Charles, Missouri, and even more different from my family that lived in Sweden or my family in South Texas. Because of my Dad's job, we were fortunate enough to travel to visit our families in Sweden, South Texas, and even Mexico. Every trip was an adventure and experience that I loved, but these experiences also made me more aware of the differences between cultures and within me. I learned to "code switch" early in life. Way earlier, before I first learned what the term meant in adulthood in a Diversity, Equity, & Inclusion (DEI) leadership class.

It was normal for me to celebrate multiple Christmas holidays. We kicked off the winter festivities celebrating St. Lucia Day, *Posadas*, Christmas, and *Día de los Reyes*. On Christmas Eve, we ate tamales, Swedish meatballs, rice pudding, and ham, but on regular days when Mom worked late, my Dad would cook us hot dogs and french fries. We had boxed cereal for breakfast before school during the week, and weekend breakfasts consisted of either European cold breakfast sandwiches or breakfast burritos. On special occasions and sleepovers, we were lucky enough to have Swedish pancakes!

I loved my home life and being part of a multicultural household. However, at school, I was the opposite of the fearless, curious, and always up for adventure kid I was at home. I was aware that I was the minority and outlier compared to my nonminority friends. I was the only Latina in school until high school. I was quiet and didn't want to draw attention to myself or my subtle differences. I have olive-toned skin, and my hair is very curly and frizzes like crazy in humid temps. Up until college, many of my school friends just assumed I was black or mixed. I didn't give much thought to my race because I had become so used to common questions such as "Where are you from?" I'd respond with "Missouri," only to get asked the follow-up question of "No, where are you *really* from?" My responses were on autopilot. "I'm from Missouri but born in Texas. I'm American. I'm Hispanic and white. My mother is from Mexico, and my dad is from Sweden." I never took offense at getting asked these questions, but it wasn't until I became a working adult that I realized my cultural background made for interesting conversation, which had the power to motivate and inspire others. I just had to find courage and find my voice to share it.

Both my parents worked full time and instilled in me a strong work ethic. Working hard allows you to play hard. I had a strong work ethic in school and carried it into the workforce when I started my career in banking. It felt like starting school all over again. I wanted to always give it my best and do a good job and be a people pleaser. I wanted to please my customers, please my managers, be a good team player, and just be liked and accepted.

At work and in school, I learned to keep my head down, get the job done, not cause conflict, and always ask for permission. This is what I believed was needed from me to thrive in the American work culture and what I thought a strong work ethic looked like. It felt purely robotic, but that's what I thought the workplace was. However, it wasn't until I moved from retail banking into corporate banking, where I was fortunate enough to be exposed to some strong and talented mentors, that my logic and assumptions were challenged. For the first time outside my home, I started to embrace diversity. Not so much physical diversity but internal diversity. Diverse thoughts, diverse opinions, and diverse ideas.

One of the best and most influential pieces of leadership advice I ever received was from my regional market executive, who was also my mentor. He said to be a leader, you must do three things: 1) Show up. 2) Engage and participate. 3) Have the courage to lead. It sounded easy and totally made sense. It wasn't something that felt natural or normal for me to do, at least until I was forced.

I remember being in a big boardroom on the twelfth floor of our corporate office. Being one of the youngest associates and a minority woman, I just wanted to fly below the radar. I showed up to the meeting five minutes before start time. Starting off, I had step one covered. I was also pretty good at step two. I nodded along with the rest of the peers and followed "groupthink," which made me feel like I was participating and engaging in the conversation, even though it was just the bare minimum.

At one point in the meeting, the market executive asked a question, and several of the senior leaders around the table gave their thoughts. I remained quiet but listened attentively. I can't exactly recall what topic was being discussed, but my boss called on me and asked me to share my thoughts. I must have disagreed or had a different thought or idea from what was said because he said I wasn't permitted to have a disagreeing look on my face without sharing my thoughts behind the look I was giving. Now it became the moment of truth, and I was to act on step three: have courage. I cleared my throat, spoke up, and shared my thoughts on why I didn't agree with the senior leader. I was being, of course, very respectful and professional. I stayed cool, calm, and collected on the outside. On the inside, I was scared to death thinking these leaders would never like me, respect me, and never would accept me.

To my surprise, several others in the room wanted to hear more about my alternative idea. Other leaders in the room who were quiet up to this point started asking questions and engaging with their thoughts. It was beautiful to see the engagement and collaboration from everyone, not just the few. I realized that it took one small spark to ignite a whole flame of creativity and discussion on the art of the possible, and I was that small spark that helped make it happen. After executing step three, I felt a huge wave of relief afterward and realized that I survived. People took me seriously and valued my perspective, so I could stop worrying about what others would think. I learned to just do it, and not ever play poker because clearly, I don't have a poker face.

The ability to be authentic and to stop worrying about what other people may think of you is a superpower because we're all different, so there's no need to compare yourself to others. There's no right way, there's no wrong way, there's just another way. There is no "normal." Like my mother said, "Normal is a setting on a dishwasher or laundry machine, and you're not a machine." It's okay to be different, and there is no need to assimilate just to fit the status quo, to what everyone else is doing around you.

I continue to abide by the three rules of leading and share them with new leaders and others I mentor within my organization. It's my own way of "paying it forward," and I strongly believe wisdom is to be shared to learn, grow, and live with authenticity.

Anita Hansen is the Relationship Team Administrator and Support Manager for Commercial Banking at Regions Bank. She graduated from Lindenwood University. As a daughter of an immigrant mother from Mexico and an immigrant father from Sweden, Anita is the first of her family to be born in the United States. Having a diverse cultural background has allowed Anita to have a strong appreciation for diversity and inclusion. She also serves as co-chair for the Regions Bank's Inclusion, Belonging, and Impact network for the St. Louis market. Anita volunteers and supports several non-profit organizations, including the Hispanic Chamber of Commerce, Regional Business Council, United Way, Junior Achievement, Arts and Education Council, Doorways, and more.

Anita is married to Jason Hansen, a leader of the band, FatPocket. Together, they have twin 12-year-old boys, Parker and Chase, and two dogs, Daisy, a Newfoundland, and Hazel, a basset hound. Anita enjoys traveling, cooking, and attending all types of music concerts with her family.

Please scan the QR code to connect with this author.

Gabriela Claudia Ochoa

To the Women Who Made Me

This is a love letter to the women who have inspired me, shaped me, held me up, and raised me, whether by blood, choice, or simply by being exactly who they are in the moments I needed them most.

I Love Women

Yes, I'm married to a man, and he is kind, steady, and wonderful, but I *love* women. Deeply. Profoundly. In a way that transcends romance and pierces the soul. There is something sacred and electric about the way women move through the world, like how we carry contradiction and truth in the same breath. We are soft and sharp, tender and unrelenting, messy and magnificent. We hold multitudes, and somehow, we still make room for more.

The women in my life, you have been my sounding boards and my sanctuaries. You've seen me not just in my best moments but in the raw, ugly, vulnerable ones too, and chose to stay. That is love. You are my soul-mates. Plural. Each of you, in your own way, knows me at my core, my truest self, even the parts I so desperately try to hide. For that, I am both endlessly grateful and, if I'm being honest, a little terrified.

This is for you. Thank you for loving me when I didn't yet love myself. Thank you for modeling grace, resilience, humor, and depth. Thank you for being the blueprint.

I carry your wisdom with me, always.

Diana. Mumsy. *Mujer.* Mom.

You were right about everything. You were right about the friendships that faded quietly and the ones that held fast through storms. You were right about the partners who didn't deserve my softness and the ones who came offering peace instead of chaos. You were right about what I was capable of, if only I would stop doubting myself and focus. You said I could do it before I even knew what it was, and you were always right.

Are you psychic? Do you have visions? Where are you hiding your third eye, and how do I get one? Because it's not just your intuition, it's your clarity. The way you see people. The way you can hear what someone isn't saying and know exactly what they need. The way you can read a room without a word being spoken.

What really amazes me isn't your foresight, it's your light. I don't understand how someone who's lived through as much as you have, who's warned me about certain heartbreaks, not from paranoia but from experience, can still be so relentlessly kind. How do you keep choosing to be openhearted when the world has given you every reason to close it off? You've shown the people around you, me especially, what unconditional love really looks like. You've also shown me its limits. You've given so much of your heart that I've learned love has to have conditions. Not because it's stingy, but because it deserves respect.

I did not inherit your patience or your gentleness. I love hard, with a clenched jaw and fists ready to defend. I guard the people I love. But you? You give grace to people who haven't even asked for it yet. You give without keeping score, and every time I try to understand how, I'm reminded that this is your strength. Still, we complement each other. We are like fire and water; firm and forgiving. I am not me without you. You taught me to stand up for what's right and still know when to stand down. You gave me your values, your beliefs, your moral compass, but you also gave me the freedom to shape them into my own.

Thank you for your tenderness, even when I didn't know how to accept it. Thank you for being soft, even when life was hard. Thank you for showing me, again and again, that loving people isn't a weakness. It's the fiercest strength of all.

I love you endlessly. And I'm still learning from you, even now.

Rebecca. Becca. Becky. Bby Grl.

You've always carried a universe inside you, wide open, unapologetic. I've yet to meet another person who feels their feelings as deeply and as freely as you do, or even laughs with the full-bodied, guttural joy that you do. You've taught me that emotion isn't something to hide from or rationalize away. To feel is to be alive. Every tear, every burst of laughter, it's all part of being human. You never edited yourself to be more "acceptable." You just were and still are. That's been more of a gift to me than you could ever know.

I remember the first time I really cried in front of someone who wasn't family. In tenth-grade English, we read *Pride and Prejudice* and, of course, watched the 2005 Keira Knightley adaptation. It was the moment Mr. Darcy walked through the morning mist and said, "I love you. Most ardently." We didn't even need to look at each other. We both knew the other was wrecked in the best way. Ugly crying in tandem over fictional people. It was then that I realized: feeling together and being open together was its own kind of freedom.

You created a space where emotions weren't liabilities, they were truths. You didn't just tolerate feelings, you honored them; yours, mine, everyone's. Even when I wasn't ready then to be as open as you were, I watched, and I learned. Slowly, piece by piece, I've started to understand the power in vulnerability. I've learned that hiding what hurts, or what lights us up, only keeps us small. You taught me that honesty can be soft and fierce. Now I see you taking that into your work, your writing, your journalism. You pull truth out into the light, not with force but with grace. You help people feel seen in a world that so often numbs or distracts, you remind us to feel. If I haven't said it lately, I'm proud of you. Proud of your bravery, your voice, and the way you keep choosing to show up.

I love you, I always have, I always will, and I can't wait to laugh and cry with you soon.

Alejandra. *Mi hermanita*. Hanna. Ale.

The perpetual pain in my backside and the permanent piece of my heart.

You are the funniest, goofiest, most pure-of-heart person I know. There's no one who can annoy me and uplift me in the same breath quite like you. As the eldest daughter, nine years your senior, I feel I must be your guide, your second mom, your semi-responsible adult figure. You make me feel like a kid again. When I'm with you, I laugh louder, smile wider, and remember deep in my bones that life is short, time is precious, and every moment is worth celebrating.

It feels like just yesterday you were still too small to reach the pedals, yet there you were, behind the wheel of the family minivan, eyes barely peering over the steering wheel, your entire body vibrating with excitement and fear and pure chaotic joy. I can still hear your laughter and screaming, not from panic but from sheer exhilaration. I watched, holding my breath, silently negotiating with the universe for your safety. I was terrified. You were thrilled.

That's always been you: brave in the weirdest, most unexpected ways. Recklessly hopeful. Laughing in the face of fear, dancing into uncertainty like it's just another joke waiting to be made. And when I find myself stuck in my own fear, unsure of which way to go, I think of you. I think of that wild look in your eye and that mischievous smirk you flash when you've had a terrible idea that you know I will desperately try to talk you out of.

You've been my little sister since the day you were born, but over the years, you've also become my teacher, my comic relief, my reminder to not take everything so damn seriously. Thank you. Thank you for being exactly who you are, for never shrinking. For never letting me forget how much fun this life can be, even when it's terrifying.

Ailey, Alice, Francine, Kayla, Neosha, Shannon, and Terry.

My sisters in service, words truly fall short when I try to express the depth of my gratitude and admiration for each of you. The work you do is nothing short of transformative. You show up for your communities with courage, love, and commitment. Your leadership is not only effective but rooted in compassion, justice, and the belief that everyone deserves a chance to thrive.

You inspire me daily to lead with heart, to listen with empathy, and never to forget who I'm doing this work for. Your resilience in the face of challenges and your passion for uplifting others continue to light my path and strengthen my purpose. I am forever grateful for your friendship, your guidance, and your belief in me. You have not only shaped the way I lead, but also the way I live. I can only hope these words come close to conveying how deeply I admire, respect, and adore each of you. Your impact on my life and on the lives of so many others is immeasurable, and I am endlessly honored to know you.

In the end, this isn't just a love letter, it's a living tribute. To the women who shaped my backbone and softened my edges, who held me up when I stumbled and reminded me who I was when I forgot. You are in every decision I make, every boundary I set, every act of love I give. I am who I am because of you. And while these words are mine, this story is ours.

Gabriela Claudia Ochoa, a San Diego native, is a proud Latina and Navy veteran whose passion for service is rooted in her upbringing.

Growing up in a working-class Mexican American family, she witnessed firsthand the challenges many communities face in accessing healthcare, education, and economic opportunity. These early experiences instilled in her a deep commitment to equity and a belief in the power of community.

Gabriela has built a career focused on expanding access to essential services and advocating for historically marginalized groups. Now based in St. Louis, she serves as network manager at the Community Impact Network, leading equity-driven initiatives across North St. Louis County. Her work is guided by a strong sense of cultural pride, justice, and the desire to create lasting change.

Gabriela lives in Webster Groves with her husband, Matthew, and their rescue dog, Cosmos.

Please scan the QR code to connect with this author.

Peggy Ray

Me Too

It was 2009, I was 19 years old, and I was working at a summer camp. A fellow counselor was sharing with me about something that had happened to her in her childhood. She couldn't quite name it, but she shared the story, and for her, it was something confusing. I listened to the story, and for the first time in my life, I acknowledged something that had been hidden in me. I looked at her and whispered, "Me too."

Let's back up a couple of weeks. I was a counselor at this camp, and I had a small group of sweet, spunky 12-year-old girls. There was one specific girl whom I struggled with in Bible study. She didn't believe in God, which was fine. That's not necessary, but she was combative and just kind of difficult, especially during Bible study. That's okay. We dealt with it, moved forward, and just tried to love her. I really cared about these campers.

One evening during worship time, she came to me crying. She was clearly struggling with these ideas we were presenting about God being a loving, kind *person* who wanted to love and know her. I will never forget her face as she looked me in the eyes and asked, "If God is real, then why didn't He protect me from being sexually abused?"

There were no words. I held her, we prayed, we cried. Later that evening, I would have to report this to child protective services and call her parents. It was something they were aware of; it had already been reported, and they were in the process of supporting her through it.

She had a clear understanding of what had happened to her, what it was called, and she held it with so much courage. It was hitting her at her core as she wrestled with some of the deeper questions of life: "Why do we suffer? Is there a God? Why does this God allow evil?"

That night, when we returned to the cabin, I got my campers into bed, being as cheery as I could. Once they were settled, I stumbled out the door. I remember that as I turned the corner of our cabin, for the first time in my life, I was so overwhelmed with grief that I collapsed to the ground weeping, weeping over this girl and her pain, over what had happened. I was completely overcome. I had never cried this hard. I had never been so consumed with grief.

I'm not in touch with that little girl, who is now grown up like me. She will probably never know the part she played in my life as I processed my own experiences.

Summer camp ended, and I returned to my junior year of college. In that first semester, a few months after that first time I said, "Me too," I tried again to make sense of these memories that I held. I said to my friend Molly, "I think as a child I was sexually…harassed?" I looked at her, expectantly, wanting her to tell me how to feel, what it was, what it all meant. I literally asked, "How should I feel?" Like a good friend, she said, "I don't know. Feel however you feel." These were my first attempts to answer the question, "What happened to me?"

Each of these little moments was part of my journey of understanding. I didn't understand, and that felt vulnerable. It was hard to share something that I felt so much shame around, but didn't even know how to define it. I held these moments in the back of my mind as I continued in school.

The second semester of that year, I met a new friend, Amanda. She was a 29-year-old mother of four. Her life was *so* different than mine. Her days were full of caring for little ones. Life was demanding, but she still had time for people outside her family. She had a lot of love to give. I wanted to be around her. I wanted to be like her.

She talked openly about her own struggles and wasn't shy that life was hard and scary sometimes. Up to this point, I was accustomed to adults "having it all together." She stopped me in my tracks when one day we were chatting and she said calmly, "Sometimes I feel like such an F-up, ya know?" I was flabbergasted. Of course, I know what you mean, but you can't *say* that. She also spoke openly about women who had experienced sexual abuse. One day, she shared with me the shocking statistic that 1 in 3 women in the U.S. have experienced sexual abuse or assault of some kind. I quickly responded, "Oh, I have!" My words were so glib and shocking that she retorted, "Nuh-uh! By who?" We laugh about that to this day because it was the most rude, unkind way to react to someone disclosing that.

It kind of made sense! I was *so* disconnected. I was still trying to figure it out! I heard her say it and I thought, "Oh, maybe that's it." I was aware of this term, sexual abuse, but I didn't know what it meant!

I knew what kind of person that might happen to, or what it might do to them, or what it says about them or their family, or what might be messed up about them if that were true. Then I met the girl who came from a well-off family, who went to camp, whose parents were aware, and they cared about her. They were heartbroken over it. That started to crumble the idea of what "sexual abuse" means. The idea of sexual abuse was still theoretical, and I had yet to reconcile it with my own memories, my experiences.

Through my relationship with Amanda, I started to put these two together. I started to see that my experience *was* sexual abuse. As I brought them together, I also had to leave behind some of my own impressions of what it means to be someone who experienced sexual abuse. My view of that person was not someone I wanted to be. I didn't want to be associated or thought of in that way.

Amanda talked about women (or men!) who had been sexually abused, with so much grace and offered them so much affection and dignity and compassion, and it was really clear that her impression was very different from mine.

We spent hours talking and working through questions like, "What does this mean?" and "Who am I?" and "Can I face this?" She gave me resources and words to define what happened to me. I began to focus on what happened and healing from that, rather than my impression of what it meant about me, or what others might think.

I *knew* what Amanda thought about me. She knew I had been sexually abused. She saw me just as I was in all of my glory as somebody with so much dignity. Knowing me as she did, she thought I was so lovely, and I felt that. Through my friendship with Amanda, and the way she was always lifting me up, I began to have the courage to face this darkness.

Fast-forward eight years to 2017, when the "Me Too" movement started to take hold in mainstream culture. I thought back to my "me too" moment in 2009. It wasn't lost on me that these had been the very words that opened the door to face my darkness. "Me too" was not just about me; it was about responding to someone else, hearing their story, and reflecting from your own experience. It was a powerful starting point for me, and for many women.

My friendship with Amanda was the next step. She took the "me too" to a deeper place of healing. I learned to sit with myself as she sat with me. I learned to cry over what was wrong as she cried with me. I learned that if I wanted to love others, I would have to let others love me. In this season, another good friend of mine was Amanda's husband, Ronnie.

Ronnie knew I wanted to love others and make a difference in the world. He encouraged me, "The people who go to the dark places in their own hearts will have the courage to go to the dark places in this world."[1] This motivated me. Over the next several years, I faced my darkness. Week after week, I went to therapy and prayed as I walked in, "Lord, help me to be brave today."

As I developed my own skill in sitting with pain, loneliness, and sadness, it became easier to sit with others, to notice when they wanted connection, when they were hurting or hiding. I learned to let myself be known, and it started to change me. Not only was I healing and growing in confidence, but I was also becoming the kind of friend that I needed so desperately.

The first time I said "me too," I didn't have the understanding or maturity to help myself, much less someone else. I longed to be a loving person who could make a positive impact in the world, but I was deeply disconnected from my own pain and fears. Since uttering those two powerful words, I have been on a journey to open myself to being known.

It has been scary. There were painful seasons of anxiety, loneliness, and deep, deep grief. I also opened up to the chance of being truly known and seen, which in turn taught me how to truly know and see others. I didn't want to be seen as someone who had been sexually abused. Now, on the other side of this, I'm not ashamed, and it's a helpful truth that doesn't define me when I say, "Me too."

---

[1] I believe this was his version of the Carl Jung quote, "Knowing your own darkness is the best method for dealing with the darknesses of other people."

Peggy Ray is a mother of three who loves to have fun and talk about ideas. She works at the Hispanic Chamber of Commerce in St. Louis, MO, where she supports professionals and businesses in the region. She is active in her church and community.

Please scan the QR code to connect with this author.

Veronica "Ronnie" Soria

Duality by Choice

I remember when I was a child, I always wanted to help others. Serving others, whether it was the kids on the block, my teachers, my mother, or the church I went to, always felt like second nature. What I didn't know at the time was that those small acts of kindness were shaping the foundation of who I would become.

I grew up in a Latino (Mexican/Puerto Rican) household where service, kindness, and resilience weren't just values; they were a way of life. I watched my parents give to others without expecting anything in return. My father would wake up at 3 a.m. to go fishing, come back, clean the fish, and by mid-morning, he would be handing out buckets of fish to all the neighbors. My mother never turned anyone away from our table. Whether we had a little or a lot, she made it stretch because, in her heart, there was always enough when it came to feeding people. Compassion was our everyday language, and I saw it in action from the moment I opened my eyes each day. That early foundation of giving and selflessness left a lasting mark on my life. I didn't fully understand it at the time, but I was being taught something important: Leadership begins with service, and strength is rooted in love.

Years later, I found myself walking a very different path, much different than the one I thought I would ever take! It was one lined with camouflage, drill formations, weapons qualifications, and combat boots. I became a United States Marine, proudly serving for 20 years. I was honored to wear the uniform and stand among warriors, but the path was not easy. The culture demanded strength, endurance, mental fortitude, and sometimes emotional armor. I had to learn to lead in a male-dominated environment where emotions were seen as weakness and compassion was misunderstood. There were times I had to suppress the softer parts of myself. I stood tall, spoke firmly, and showed up with tenacity. But deep down, I wrestled with a question that many women in high-pressure roles ask themselves: Do I have to become a hardened soul to be taken seriously?

When I was serving as a drill instructor on Parris Island, it was then that I eventually discovered my strength lay not in denying my softness but in owning it. I was told to stop being compassionate, but I stood my ground and stated that I would not change who I was; instead, I would lead with it. This was the first time I embraced the compassionate, loving human being I was. I found that the power of leading from a place of empathy, intuition, and care was not a liability. It was my edge. I didn't have to be either/or. I could be both…and I was, and I am! I lead with both compassion and command presence. I am a strong decision-maker and a safe place for someone to fall apart. I realized that the very things I thought I had to hide—such as my emotional sensitivity, nurturing nature, and faith—were the same things that allowed me to connect, inspire, and build trust in ways that others could not. This duality of being a hard-core Marine and a deeply loving, compassionate woman became not only my reality but my superpower. It taught me one of the most profound lessons I've ever learned: True strength is found in balance. And discovering that truth changed the course of my leadership and my life.

Courage, I learned, isn't just about being fearless or taking charge when someone is needed. It's also about showing up with grace in hardship. It's the quiet resilience of a woman who's been broken and still chooses to heal. It's the strength to lead through doubt and the gentleness to sit in silence with someone who's hurting. I have led in environments where I had to maintain a hardened posture, and others where my compassion was readily apparent. Those moments in my service when I had no choice but to adopt a hardened posture, mission and safety came first, and emotions had to be locked away.

I recall one operation, during a money run in another country, when I rode in a military vehicle carrying a large sum of cash. As we rolled down the major highway, we found ourselves side by side with a known terrorist group. In that moment, my entire mind and body shifted; I was alert, calm, but fully ready to protect the money, my troops, and myself. There was no room for fear or softness, only focus, command, and unwavering bravery. And yet, that same uniform also called for compassion.

I once had a young troop who had gotten into serious trouble and was facing discharge. Others had already written him off, choosing to walk away rather than invest in someone they felt had failed. But I saw him. I pulled him into my section, gave him responsibility, and told him, "I'm going to teach you what grace looks like." I made it clear he was still accountable for his actions, but I also wanted him to leave the Marine Corps with his head held high and a new understanding of his worth. Leadership demanded both sides of me, disciplined and discerning, tough and tender. Both experiences have left their mark on me. Both have made me who I am.

I faced many hardships throughout my life journey. I know how it feels to be underestimated, overlooked, and misunderstood. I know what it means to carry invisible wounds while showing up every day with purpose. And I have genuinely come to see the freedom that comes from doing the deep inner work to heal, forgive, and move forward stronger. There is a unique power that comes from walking through traumatic experiences and not letting them harden you, from letting those scars tell a story instead of hiding them. I am a survivor, and that's what drives me to help others rise!

Today, I serve in a different way but with the same mission. I've taken everything I've learned from my years of military service, my coaching, leadership development, and my life experience. I use my experiences to create spaces where people can pause, reflect, and reignite their purpose. My heart is for those women like me who are navigating a storm. For the one questioning if her softness has a place in a complicated world, for the woman who's tired of choosing between strength and grace. I want women to know that they are more powerful than they know.

We never have to choose between being strong and being soft. We do not have to trade our compassion for credibility. We can be both. We were created to be resilient! The world may try to convince us to toughen up, to hide our feelings, to power through without rest, but I want all women to know that our softness is not a weakness. It is sacred. Our nurturing heart, our empathy, and our instinct to serve and protect are not defects. They are our superpowers.

We need to permit ourselves to be fierce and gentle, structured and soulful, resilient and radiant. We are shaped and molded by our experiences, bringing in a blend of strength and love. Every scar we have holds a sacred story. Every tear we've shed has watered the roots of our strength.

We are not just surviving. We are becoming. We are becoming the woman who leads with her whole heart. The woman who doesn't shrink to fit in but stands tall in her truth. The woman who gives herself permission to feel, to grow, to fall down, and to reclaim her strength. We were never meant to walk this journey alone. And we were never meant to become someone else to be worthy. We are already enough.

My experience is just one example, but if it serves as a reminder to just one woman that healing is possible, that leadership looks many different ways, and that it's okay to embrace every layer of who you are, then it was worth sharing. We are not meant to live in pieces. We are meant to lead from a place of wholeness. Wholeness comes when we honor who we are: the grit that keeps us going and the grace that keeps us grounded. Keep walking gracefully, boldly, and fully!

The world needs women like us.

Women who lead from the places they've overcome.

Women who carry both fire and light.

Women who are not afraid to be soft in a world that demands toughness.

Women who know that vulnerability is strength, and healing is holy.

You are that woman.

And I see you.

Veronica Soria is a retired United States Marine who proudly served for 20 years. She continued her passion for developing others in the federal government as a learning and development consultant, program manager for the institution's Aspiring Leaders Program, leadership development coach, and speaker. Veronica holds an M.A. in Education and Human Behavior, an M.Ed. in Training and Development, and a B.S. in Psychology. She is the founder of MVS Solutions LLC, where she helps individuals and organizations grow through purpose-driven coaching and training. Veronica blends real-life experience with professional insight to create safe spaces for reflection, healing, and transformation. Known for her nurturing spirit and unshakable integrity, she brings heart to every conversation and believes in the power of grace, accountability, and personal growth. Veronica's mission is simple yet profound: to help others rediscover their strength, embrace their story, and step boldly into their purpose. She is an author in the *Camouflaged Sisters Stories of Strength and Resilience in the Military Transition* (2024) and the *Camouflaged Sisters Strength in Service Inspirational Devotional* (2025).

Please scan the QR code to connect with this author.

Athena K. Ramos

A Serendipitous *Bendición*

Bendición means "blessing" in Spanish, but for Puerto Ricans, like me, the word *"bendición"* is something deeper than a simple blessing. It is a greeting and a farewell when you see family and friends. It is a sentiment that encompasses both love and respect, representing a sacred exchange between two people, one that grounds them, connects them, and reminds them of who they are and what really matters in life.

When I think about lifting others as I climb, I have to first express my gratitude to someone who helped me to climb—a special person who supported my journey and taught me invaluable lessons about leadership and life.

It was 2002 when I first met Antonia. We both worked on a grant-funded project that focused on reducing tobacco use and preventing exposure to secondhand smoke in the Latino community. She worked for the university, and I worked for the Latino Center. I was only 21, newly graduated from college, and starting my career. I had no idea where this relationship would lead or how deeply it would take root. Antonia had moved to Omaha a few years prior at the age of 49, from Puerto Rico, where she had been a professional counselor. Many people looked at us and wondered about our ability to work together, questioning, "How can you work with her?" because of such a difference in age and life experience.

From educating youth on the dangers of tobacco to going door-to-door down the street, engaging with business owners to establish smoke-free policies, we did amazing things! We worked together fluidly because we had a joint passion for people and a *compromiso* with the community. Plus, we shared a deep respect for one another. Our relationship linked Antonia's life experience and wisdom with my energy and creativity.

Antonia and I became not only colleagues but serendipitously best friends. She helped me understand my self-worth at a time when I wanted to be everything that I wasn't. Like other young women, I wanted to be prettier, taller, skinnier, smarter, and change my hair color, eye color, skin color, you name it. I didn't like what I saw on the outside. But the physical body didn't matter to Antonia; she focused on the inside. She could see my heart. Through her consistent *cariño*, I came to realize that I was enough. I didn't need to change anything about myself to be valued or worthy of love.

In 2007, a career opportunity for a supervisory position arose at the university in Antonia's department. She encouraged me to apply for the job, and I got it! Technically, I became her boss. Coming into a management position at the age of 26 in an academic institution was challenging, to say the least. People doubted my knowledge, skills, and ability to be an effective manager. Not Antonia. She believed in me even when I didn't believe in myself.

Although some might have thought that because we were friends, we were going to just hang out all day. They were wrong. Nothing could be further from the truth. It was because of our friendship that we worked even harder. We understood each other's work and communication styles, motivations, and could hear what wasn't being said. Neither of us wanted to let the other down. Together, we were ambitious, and we gave life to projects that some believed were impossible. We founded the *Latinas, Tabaco, y Cancer* group, a culturally tailored women's health promotion and support group that is now over 20 years old. We hosted the first Spanish-language women's health conference in Nebraska, *El Encuentro de La Mujer Sana*, in 2013, bringing together Latina women from both Omaha and Lincoln. This model for a Latina women's health conference has now been implemented by non-profit organizations in at least three other communities spanning the state of Nebraska. We also launched the first research study on Latino migrant farmworker health in the state. We didn't do any of this for recognition or self-promotion. We did all of this to create opportunities for others to grow, to be visible, and to improve the conditions of people's lives.

I was hungry to do more and have an even greater impact on the people and communities we served, but in an academic setting, a terminal degree is necessary to open doors. I knew what I had to do. I applied for and was accepted into a PhD program. This was the key to unlocking opportunities, but it definitely wasn't easy. I was working full-time, going to school full-time, and trying my best to be a good Mom to three kids. A PhD can be a lonely endeavor, always being in your head thinking or in some corner reading, but I found solace in Antonia. She would fuel my study habits with delicious homemade Puerto Rican food like *arroz*, *habichuelas*, and *chuletas*. She really knew the way to my heart! She would bring me Panera treats, pumpkin coffees, and lots of chocolate. We would talk over concepts discussed in classes, self-care, and mental health.

Even though I had been raised to be independent and tough, I began to see that it was alright to show emotions and that I didn't always have to be ok. I grew up in a family where there wasn't a lot of talk about feelings. As a kid, I was just expected to follow instructions, not to ask questions. Asking for help, as you might imagine, had never been my strong suit. With Antonia, though, I didn't need to ask. She already knew, and she jumped in to help with whatever she could, both at the office and on the home front.

I became Dr. Athena Ramos in 2017, building my dissertation on the foundational work that Antonia and I had done with migrant farmworkers. Nobody tells you how much your life will change with those three extra letters, PhD, behind your name. At least, I guess I never got the warning. It was almost as if the switch had been flipped entirely. It was an incredible feeling to be Dr. Ramos, but also quite daunting and sometimes overwhelming, especially when I thought about how few Latinas have completed a doctoral degree.

I bid farewell, professionally, to Antonia in 2018 as she retired from my team, but to me, she is the epitome of a woman supporting other women. She invested in me and so many others. She taught me about the power of accompaniment and being present—from literally walking down the street together to walking alongside me through my career, marriage, the birth of my four kids, the grief of losing my Daddy, graduate studies, and throughout life. She taught me about empathy and caring for people in a way that I have never experienced from anyone else, through enduring love, unconditional support, and friendship. She taught me a way of being, seeing, doing, and living that valued human dignity and built community. Together, Antonia and I planted many seeds that have borne much fruit. Antonia has been a *bendición* in my life, as a colleague, a friend, a mentor, a good partner, like a second mother, and now, as my *comadre* and godmother to my daughter, Italia.

Over the years, I have climbed high in academia, rising from a program coordinator to a program manager, to an instructor, then assistant professor, and now as an associate professor. I have climbed higher than I think I ever could have imagined, especially since neither of my parents had gone to college. In the United States, only 2.5% of university associate professors, like me, are Latinas. I lead a scientific research and outreach team that focuses on the health and well-being of people who work in the agrifood system—the people who put food on our tables—from the corn fields, to cattle feedlots, to meatpacking plants, and beyond. I have the honor of being able to invest in people and communities that are often invisible or forgotten. Climbing high is not really about me as an individual. It's about being able to unlock resources and open pathways for others. It's about giving voice to the stories that people share with me. It's about intentionally welcoming others, fostering a sense of belonging, and building communities where everyone has an opportunity to thrive, both on- and off-campus. It's about being able to make a difference in people's lives and do good.

As a university professor, I have the privilege and the responsibility to support others as they rise. I get to invest in those who want to learn, who want to spark positive change, and who have that same passion for community and justice that I do. On my team now, I have people who started with me as master's degree students, transitioned to full-time professional staff members upon graduation, and who are now pursuing PhDs. Others came directly into full-time positions on my team with an undergraduate degree and now have or are in the process of completing their master's degrees in public health. Eight women, including four Latinas, have chosen me to support them through their doctoral studies and invited me to either serve on or chair their dissertation committees. I try to give them my best, and I believe in them even when they sometimes doubt themselves. Life has really come full circle.

There's so much to pass along, not just discipline-specific knowledge but also life lessons as I walk alongside my students, mentees, colleagues, and community members. I carry with me all that I have learned from Antonia and honor her legacy in the day-to-day interactions that I have with everyone. I try to ensure that they experience the care and support that I have felt over the years. I share my stories of self-doubt, impostor syndrome, successes, challenges, and the importance of expressing feelings, showing our own humanity, and not putting off the important things outside the classroom or the office. We work hard and grow professionally and personally through collaboration. We laugh together, and sometimes, we cry together too. We share food. From new jobs to *bodas*, babies, and everything in between, we share life. I learn as much from all the people in my circle as they learn from me, if not more. I am blessed to have the opportunity to be a part of their lives, and I can only hope that I will be that *bendición* for others as they climb.

By lifting others as we climb, we help others grow, thrive, and carry the work forward. We plant seeds hoping they land in fertile soil and flourish. My story illustrates how one relationship—a sacred exchange rooted in love, mutual respect, intergenerational percipience, and shared purpose—nourished my soul and transformed my life. It shows that good that is sown can multiply exponentially, across generations, impacting the trajectories of both individuals and communities. For me, the word *bendición* is both literal and symbolic, rich with intention and visible through presence, action, and legacy.

Dr. Athena Ramos is a wife, mother, and global citizen dedicated to building healthier, more inclusive, and vibrant communities. An accomplished public health leader and scholar, she focuses on the well-being of agrifood system workers, Latinos, and rural populations. She is an associate professor in the Department of Health Promotion at the University of Nebraska Medical Center's College of Public Health and is affiliated with the Center for Reducing Health Disparities and the Central States Center for Agricultural Safety and Health. Nationally recognized for her work in farmworker health and social justice, Dr. Ramos leads innovative, community-based initiatives addressing occupational health, mental health, and chronic disease prevention. Her work blends academic rigor with deep cultural insight and a commitment to equity. A sought-after speaker and facilitator—from TEDx stages to international forums—she brings energy, authenticity, and hope to every endeavor. Dr. Ramos has received numerous awards for her leadership, service, and research excellence.

Please scan the QR code to connect with this author.

Syerra Meadows-Haynes

When Morning Breaks: Rising Through Loss

The call came in the stillness of early morning, and with it, my world shifted. My father was gone. The news felt surreal, as though I were floating outside myself, watching life unfold from a distance. My heart ached with the weight of finality, yet I knew that grief would not wait.

One of the best memories I have of my dad is that he was my softball coach. My father was a natural athlete. He played basketball and baseball for years in community leagues, and I used to love watching him on the court and field, always one of the best players on the team. When I started developing an interest in softball during my freshman year of high school, it was only natural that I'd lean on him, not just to show me the ropes, but to be my practice partner, my strategist, and my biggest cheerleader. We'd talk through different positions I played and ways to sharpen my skills. He taught me how to be resilient, how to bounce back after an injury, and how to keep pushing forward despite my ongoing struggles with severe asthma. But he wasn't just my coach in sports; he taught me how to drive, helped shape my taste in music, and guided me in countless other ways that molded the woman I am today.

I can still picture one practice as clearly as if it happened yesterday. We were in the middle of a scrimmage, and I had just struck out. The sting of it hit hard, not just because I missed the ball, but because I felt like I had missed the mark altogether. I was wheezing, frustrated, and overwhelmed. My asthma was flaring up, my confidence was tanking, and I could feel the eyes of the other players on me. Embarrassed and discouraged, I ripped off my helmet, stormed over to the bench, and sank, holding back tears. At that moment, I was ready to quit, not just the game, but the belief that I belonged on that field at all.

Then my dad walked over. He didn't raise his voice or offer a pep talk laced with clichés. Instead, he knelt beside me, his presence calm and steady. He looked me in the eyes and said gently, *"Don't let one moment define your whole game."* Just eight words, but they landed like truth I didn't know I needed. Without saying much more, he picked up my glove, handed it to me, and nodded toward the field. *"Next inning's coming. Let's go."*

That was my dad's way of lifting me up. He didn't coddle me, but he never left me in my discouragement either. He saw my strength even when I couldn't, and he knew how to pull it out of me—without force, without pressure, just belief. That day, and so many others like it, he taught me one of the most important lessons of my life: to keep showing up, even when it hurts, especially when it hurts.

The first few days after my father passed were a blur, filled with silent grieving, whispered prayers, and an overwhelming weight I couldn't fully put into words. I cried quietly in stolen moments, tucking my own sorrow away as I focused on helping my mother begin to process the unimaginable and take the first steps toward a life without him. My father had been the anchor of our family. His love, strength, and unwavering guidance had shaped not only my values but my faith journey. Without him, I felt unmoored, like a ship drifting without direction, trying to find stability in a sea of sorrow while holding everyone else together.

One verse that held me together during that time was Psalm 34:18: "The Lord is close to the brokenhearted and saves those who are crushed in spirit." In the most crushing season of my life, I felt God draw near—not to take away the pain, but to steady me in it. His presence didn't erase the ache, but it wrapped around me like a quiet strength, giving me the peace I didn't have the words to ask for.

My faith shifted in the aftermath of his passing. It grew deeper, quieter, and more honest. In those first weeks, my prayers were less structured and more like survival cries: *"Why now?" "How am I supposed to keep going?"* Over time, they became prayers of surrender: *"Hold me, Lord. Use this pain. Teach me through it."* Grief stripped away the polished parts of my faith and left me with only what was real. I stopped trying to impress God with strength I didn't have and started trusting Him with weakness I could no longer hide. I learned that He doesn't require perfect prayers, just honest ones. In that rawness, I began to heal.

Even as I grieved, I had to find a way to keep going. My daughter needed me. Her eyes searched mine for reassurance, her spirit still full of life and light. In many ways, she became my reason to keep rising each day. She reminded me that even in the deepest sorrow, there is still joy to be found, still purpose to fulfill. Caring for her meant I couldn't stay buried in my grief. I had to show up, not just for her but for myself.

In that space—where pain and peace coexisted—I began to sense something more stirring within me. A deeper calling. As I leaned into my faith, I realized how many women might be walking a similar path: grieving, trying to find their way through the loss of a father. Some might not have the foundation of faith I was clinging to, or the support system I had around me. The thought stayed with me: *Who walks with them?*

That's when God began to whisper something new into my heart: that this pain, as devastating as it was, could become purpose. That I could stand in the gap for those women, offering comfort, community, and a reminder that faith can hold us when everything else feels like it's falling apart.

My father's loss taught me that grief is not something we conquer but something we learn to carry. It changes us, shapes us, and, if we allow it, can deepen our compassion and sense of purpose. I began to see my pain not as a barrier but as a bridge, an opportunity to connect with other women who had lost their fathers.

What has sustained me most on this journey is the unwavering belief that God never wastes our pain. Romans 8:28 reminds us that "in all things God works for the good of those who love Him." I cling to that promise, trusting that even in the heartbreak of losing my father, God is working something meaningful, something bigger than I can yet understand.

Through my own experience, I've come to see that grief isn't something we get over: it's something we learn to live through. And while it can be heavy and overwhelming, there are ways to move through it with grace and strength. One of those ways is letting your children help you heal. My daughter's presence reminded me that even in the darkest moments, there is still light. Her laughter, her innocence, and her need for me pulled me out of the depths when I wanted to disappear. She didn't just depend on me; I needed her, too.

Another way is leaning deeply into faith, allowing God to be your anchor when everything else feels uncertain. If you have faith, hold onto it with everything you have. If you're still figuring out what you believe, or if you're unsure, I encourage you to lean into a community of believers. Surround yourself with people who will pray with you, walk beside you, and remind you that hope is not lost, even when it feels like everything else is.

One of the greatest lessons my coach, my dad, taught me was resilience. He showed me what it meant to push through when things got hard. As someone who battled severe asthma, I faced limitations that sometimes made me question whether I could keep up with the sport I was falling in love with. But my dad never let me sit in discouragement.

He reminded me that setbacks weren't stop signs, just detours. His voice echoed through every challenge: *"You've got this. Just keep breathing, keep swinging."* That mindset went beyond the softball field. It showed up later in life—in classrooms, in motherhood, in leadership, and especially in grief. When he passed, I found myself drawing on that same resilience he spent years building in me.

As part of my own healing, I've started to walk more intentionally in my calling with resilience. Through honest conversations, gatherings rooted in compassion, and faith-led encouragement, I am committed to supporting women who are grieving their fathers. I want them to know that they are not alone, that their pain matters, and that there is healing—real, soul-deep healing—through God's love and the strength of community.

Losing my father changed me in ways I'm still discovering. It brought me to my knees, but it also lifted my eyes toward heaven. In this tension between sorrow and hope, I've found a new purpose: to be a vessel of encouragement and faith for women who are carrying the weight of loss.

My father's legacy lives on, not just in the memories we shared, but in the way his life inspires me to serve others. This journey has taught me that even in our brokenness, God can create something beautiful. As I continue to rise, I'm committed to lifting others with me, one step of faith at a time.

I envision rooms filled with women grieving, healing, and rising together. I envision conversations over coffee where stories are shared, tears are honored, and faith is reignited. I want to build spaces where women who've lost their fathers can come as they are and know they are held in love, in truth, and in community. My mission is not to fix their grief but to walk with them through it, to remind them that their story doesn't end with loss. It continues in love, in purpose, and in the power of sisterhood rooted in faith.

Syerra Meadows-Haynes is a dedicated community builder, youth development advocate, and faith-driven encourager. She serves as a key leader with East Side Aligned, where she supports collective impact strategies and provides capacity-building and technical assistance to youth-serving organizations across the region. Syerra is passionate about helping teams grow in their effectiveness, sustainability, and impact on young people's lives. She extends her commitment to equity and youth empowerment through board service with Eye Thrive, bringing vision care directly to children, and as strategic partnerships chair for Friends of St. Louis Public Schools, fostering school-community collaboration. Syerra is also the founder of Striving Envision Photography, capturing moments that reflect connection and purpose. A proud mother and wife, she now walks alongside women who have lost their fathers, offering faith-led encouragement and healing. She believes in rising through adversity and helping others do the same, one relationship at a time.

Please scan the QR code to connect with this author.

Chaplain Lisa Northway, U.S. Army

Mission *Amiga* Mindset: Rising with Your *Amigas*

Two people are better off than one, for they can help each other succeed.
If one person falls, the other can reach out and help.
But someone who falls alone is in real trouble!
—Ecclesiastes 4:9-10 (NLT)

Brene Brown states in *The Positivity Blog*, "Vulnerability is not winning or losing; it's having the courage to show up and be seen when we have no control over the outcome." This sets the stage for us to be able to ask for what we need, even when the preferred outcome seems impossible. In my work of advocacy for others, I can easily miss the singular brave act of self-compassion and connection to my need for others to stand with me in providing their power of presence. I make room for the possibility of better outcomes in my world, not just in the worlds of others. This is also what I define as having a *"Mission Amiga Mindset."* How do we develop a process of building a mindset that helps us rise with our *amigas*? Come along with me, *amigas* (and *amigos*), as I discuss circumstances of places where I am typically called upon to be with those who find themselves in undesirable places, many not of their own choosing. As you read on, may you resonate with images of where you could further develop your own Mission *Amiga* Mindset.

Late winter of this year, I was serving as the Garrison Chaplain of a military installation. The leader of our military team decided to move half the team to one chapel and the other half to a different military chapel, except for one office...mine. The soldier assigned with me and I were left on an entire floor of a 100-year-old historic building, although we only occupied the same offices we had worked out of for over two years.

Six months prior, we had been given a satellite office in another chapel, but without internet or a printer, so we rarely used it. My co-located teammate was also given a second satellite office at one of the other chapels, intended to be his permanent one once my replacement arrived later in the summer. From the moment the rest of the team moved to the other chapels, we regularly had realtors show the area to their visitors, asking many questions about the functionality of the old building.

By the end of April, one of those visitors came by to ask us why we were still there, as they needed me to vacate my office first so they could move in a whole section, along with the rest of their team, to inhabit the rest of the second floor. I told him I would inform our Garrison Planning Team right away to learn when and where we were moving. I was promptly informed by a Garrison Planning Team member that I wasn't moving unless he told me directly that we were moving. It suddenly seemed we were caught in a real estate war. This is not what I thought I signed up for, in service to God and country. I can say for certain I've found myself in the middle of far more workplace/real estate skirmishes, conflicts, and wars than I have been on actual combat deployments!

The next morning, the Garrison Planning Team member called back to ask me why I was still in the building. "Chaplain, you've been briefing at staff call for weeks that the Religious Support Office moved to chapels! So why are you still there?" "Yes, sir," I replied. "I also made sure to brief that Sergeant and I were left behind and are still in place." The next call I received was from the Garrison Commander telling me I needed to be out of the building in three working days. I gently reminded him that we had been proactive in providing various courses of action to the Command Sergeant Major, as requested, regarding potential relocation options, but we had yet to be given a key or access to our next place of duty. I also agreed that we would be ready to make the move.

We notified our Team Leader and Senior Non-Commissioned Officer in Charge (NCOIC). He told us he would plan on getting soldiers to help with the move on Monday. Meanwhile, I cancelled my weekend plans because my husband was out of town and not available for some of our usual teamwork required for such moves. I asked a faithful, *amiga*, a leader in our Native American community, whom I have come to trust in my current assignment, if she could join me at my office for an afternoon of light packing in advance of the move. She brought her two granddaughters along, whom I gladly paid for their meticulous packing. I think I heard every title of each book from my bookshelves called out that Sunday afternoon. We managed to pack up 75 percent of the items needing to be moved and filled up my car with items I was unsure I'd have room for, depending on where I would be relocated in the coming week. This was not the first time my cherished *amiga* gladly adjusted her schedule and packed up her grandchildren to help me complete a mission for a critical deadline.

Earlier in the weekend, two older friends who are leaders in the *American Veterans' Supporters* organization discovered I had to make a sudden office move and offered to assist. I politely declined and told them I would need them to sign up in the Volunteer Management Information System (VMIS) before I could receive their assistance. These community leaders are notable professional volunteers in the greater community, and quite frankly, I wanted to make certain they got the credit they deserved, including possible recognition in the future. On Monday afternoon, they were at Army Community Service to enroll in VMIS with the intent that they wanted to serve with the Family Life Chaplain Counseling Center. I was already dual-hatted as both the Garrison Chaplain and Family Life Chaplain since the beginning of the year, and I was anticipating building up a non-existent center that functionally disappeared when all the moves to the two chapels previously occurred. I was also informed on Monday morning that the building we thought we were moving to was now not available, so we were unable to conduct the required "urgent" move.

Tuesday morning came, and my two newest volunteers showed up at the old historic building to get to work. At 8:53, they texted me and told me they were in my office. "You mean you are downstairs waiting for me to let you in?" I replied. "No. We're upstairs in your office!" They sent a screenshot to prove it, and I stated I would be right there.

As I climbed the two flights of stairs, with the screenshots of my empty office fresh in my mind, I tried to remain calm. Surely there must be some mistake, some explanation, I thought. Like thick, dark family secrets, a cohesive answer has yet to materialize for this situation. No one would ever step up to take personal or professional responsibility for actions taken. As an Army leader, I knew I had to try to get some sort of resolution for what I believed was at risk. In my 37 years of military history, I couldn't recall one leader, apart from a death or investigation, to whom something of this nature occurred. This would be the death of a trust. Still, I was about to comprehend the deeper meaning of *Mission Amiga Mindset*, setting me up for many more months of a powerful presence that enabled me to faithfully engage in many more unenviable missions.

Sure enough, I entered my already open office, completely empty of both my personal and professional belongings. The one comfort was the presence of my two new retiree volunteers on their first day to report. They described the person who ushered them into my empty office. My mind still couldn't make sense of it. I tried not to draw attention to my biggest concern—that the confidential files in a cabinet, I quietly prayed, had not been tampered with. I knew the protocol, and as I momentarily thought through the leadership calls I needed to make, my retired chief warrant officer volunteer exclaimed aloud, "This is not the Army I served in!"

Instead of calling the Military Police to report the invasion and missing items, I contacted my First Sergeant to help me make sense of the discovery. Eventually, he confirmed that a team member failed to inform anyone of his intent and requested my assistant to help him before duty hours to relocate my belongings to an undisclosed and unsecured area. Later, my assistant and I met with our supervisor, and I relayed that the deputy garrison commander had inquired if I had received an apology. I relayed to him that I told her I hadn't asked for one. Our supervisor stated, "If she thinks you deserve an apology, then she doesn't understand the situation. My assistant pointed out my consistent reputation for rising early, even just to provide breakfast to the team if an early work call was required. I remarked that I wasn't given the opportunity to participate in the process, nor was I informed of what would take place that alarming morning. For over 37 years, I have served in an organization where mutual respect and honor are core values. Unfortunately, like other communities around the world, those values are not always embodied by each of our community members. Dutch poet, Ehsan Segal writes, "When trust is broken, there is not any medicine to recover that again, even if you try hard to gain it back."

The *undesirable gift* of the shock and awe of this unanticipated situation is that two of the most trustworthy people in my community, unrecruited by me, felt compelled to be present that horrific day. It changed the trajectory of how I was able to calmly and methodically respond to an uncommon workplace environment where trust is so essential. More than ever, I am readily proactive in asking for what I need and what I believe is essential for me and any team I'm a part of. Not because I will always receive it, but rather so I won't regret that I didn't ask to be better off. I have no doubt that if those two *comrades of character* had not been present that day, my ability to faithfully *re-engage* my mission would have been further and unnecessarily challenged. May we be people who humble ourselves to see our need to be in the company of great and trustworthy Warrior Companions our whole life long. For certain, that is key for all of us rising with our *amigas*!

Wisdom literature from my faith tradition states, "*Do all that you can to live in peace*" (Romans 12:18). We each get a vote on how we respond to conflict. Our response is our responsibility.

My chaplain blessing for all of us, dear reader, I pray, is that we take hold of all the resources we need for ourselves, our loved ones, and our comrades all our lives. I offer a prayer according to my faith tradition that it may be of encouragement today:

Dear Heavenly Father, you know my thoughts and concerns. Please reveal to me anything I still need to trust you with regarding my past, present, or future. May the enemy of my soul be kept from weaponizing my situation to shame me. When there is grief in my life, help me to also make room for your gift of joy. I choose to trust you to reveal and reconcile situations for my good and your glory over my lifetime.

May we each consider the seemingly irreparable situations of our lives, even to include broken trusts, to offer something of extra-added value to us both in the moment, and over our lifetimes. May we see the power of our presence for someone who may or may not have the courage or forethought to request our power of presence and stability, we can offer, as well as ask for the same among trusted *amigas*. With every opportunity, we can find ourselves **on mission** and **rising with our amigas**!

Chaplain Lisa Northway has been a member of the U.S. Army Chaplaincy for 37 years. She has served as a chaplain assistant, chaplain candidate, and finally as a chaplain since 2005. She has been a Family Life chaplain since 2016. She is married to Garrett, a director of religious education for the U.S. Army.

Please scan the QR code to connect with this author.

Leticia Salaro Telles

Disconnect to Reconnect with Myself

I believe we are in this world for a reason, and we do better when we are together. *Amigas Rising* caught my attention because I saw a genuine interest in doing something with a purpose…together. This is music to my ears and speaks directly to my life goal to encourage and empower others. The story of my life has some parts that need to be shared. I spent time revisiting some memories that I hid so well or never knew were there. As I allowed myself to get in touch with them, I realized I am not that Lety in my twenties or thirties anymore. I approached my memories as the person I am today. These encounters make me wonder about the many things I accomplished in life that I was not even aware of, or even make me think: How did I do that? I am going to revisit these memories with joy and pride, because they are part of who I am, and it was the best I could do in the moment that they happened. I invite you to accompany me on this journey, and I hope you can enjoy it. Let's begin!

The year was 2010. My husband arrived home from work very thrilled, because his boss offered him an assignment abroad, to spend the next four years in New York City. I could not feel more excited for him, and living in New York was not something that happens every day. When I arrived at work the following day and told my bosses what was about to happen to my husband, their reactions were not the most supportive.

I saw their faces, and my excitement turned into worry. I was a recently promoted human resources professional, involved in important projects in the international company I worked for. I had a lot of challenges and learning opportunities. I was happy. I loved my life! I needed to make a tough decision between my career and life abroad. I bet it sounds familiar to some of you, right?

It was so hard to communicate my decision at work; I was afraid to disappoint the ones who were counting on me. I did it and it was liberating! That decision was made with joy and pride. It was the right time and the right move for me and my husband in our lives as a newlywed couple. I found support in my family and friends, and the excitement started to grow again. The Frank Sinatra song never left my playlist for the following months, which gave me the strength to navigate the turbulent waters while I was preparing for the new chapter of my life.

I arrived in the Big Apple in June of 2010. It was summertime. The city was vibrant, diverse, and fun. I thought I was living in a movie! When the fall kicked off, the scenery in the city was beautiful with the foliage changing colors. I was full of hope to find a job in human resources and continue my career, as my boss wisely advised me: "Please, do not stop." When winter came, the days got shorter, and sunshine was rare. I couldn't find a job, and people did not understand what I said in English. They could not say my name, and I couldn't make new friends. That was new for me. I missed my family, my job, my life, myself. I was losing my light.

It took a few months for me to find joy again, learning to be by myself. As the job opportunities were scarce, we decided to re-route. It was a perfect time to start a family. Motherhood filled my days with joy and worries. Becoming a mother in a foreign country was a lonely journey and one of the most challenging moments in my life. Not being able to share the experiences with my family was hard. FaceTime calls every day were not enough. I had no frame of reference for a virtual baby shower. I felt even more isolated when I looked around and there was no one like me, or any familiar face, in the small suburban town I lived in. When my baby was born, I was learning how to be a mom and explore the city with a little one. I encountered many judgmental eyes in the community as I went to a coffee shop or even the grocery store.

I dedicated almost thirteen years to being a mom full-time. Three years in New York, four in Mexico City, and five in St. Louis. My children are my life! I love them dearly. I learned by myself how to be a mom. I did not have a village to help me. I had to build my village. In New York, it was hard. I had one dear friend, and we shared special moments and supported each other. In Mexico City, I found a group of women who were going through the same experiences as I was. I felt welcomed and cared for. Finding these connections with inspiring women brought my hope and joy back. I found parts of me that I loved: fun, productivity, confidence, student, mom, wife, friend, professional, artist, and athlete. I had my own village. I found my friends.

The move to St. Louis was not easy for me and for my kids. The years in Mexico were magical, and to leave our friends behind was painful. While my husband was at work, I was at home, trying to make the transition to new schools, a new house, and a new neighborhood as smooth as possible for the kids. It took a while for them to adapt. While I was worried about my children, I did not notice what was happening to me, as always. They come first, of course. The courage to touch on how this process was for me came after speaking with one of my best friends. She noticed something was different with me. I was living my life on automatic, just to attend to my children's agendas. I had no social life, I had no time for myself, and even more, I felt it was wrong to do something for myself because I needed to be there for my kids. What if they need me? Life in St. Louis was not easy in the beginning. It took years for me to adapt. The process was lonely and isolating, even though St. Louis is a great place to live, especially with children. The parts of me I found in Mexico City, I was losing again. I was not happy.

One day, I decided to participate in an event for women in the Brazilian community in St. Louis, and I met a very inspiring friend. Susan Gobbo introduced me to the International Spouses group and the International Mentoring Program. I immediately connected and started to go to the meetings and events. Finding other women who were living in St. Louis as expats seemed familiar to me. I had lost my village in Mexico, but I could join another in St. Louis. Finding new friends made me leave my hopeless self to start making plans. I met women with many different backgrounds, from many different places in the world. I was fascinated. They inspired me to reconnect to a part of myself that was lost for so long that I never thought it was possible to find it again. I was also inspired to start psychotherapy, which allowed me to untangle many of the knots I accumulated in life, in my journey to caring for myself.

I believe that building a network is powerful. It makes you feel supported, included, and confident. It helps you adapt to a new place, to a new stage of your life, to a new beginning. It was because of my network that I found the courage to start my life project, which I began in 2010 after deciding to pause my career to embrace life abroad. I have a bachelor's in psychology, and my life plan when I was in my twenties was to have a private practice as a therapist when I was in my forties. In my mind, the path to achieve that was going to be linear and smooth. I did not know that I needed to live in three different countries and twelve different homes to achieve that. In 2023, I became a graduate student at Webster University's Master's in Clinical Mental Health Counseling Program. In 2024, I started to work with immigrants in the St. Louis area as a counselor intern. In December of 2025, I will finish the program and become a PLPC (Provisional Licensed Professional Counselor). It took me a while to take one step in this direction, but I am certain that the time was just right. I needed to find my village first to start reconnecting with myself.

Hello! I am Leticia: mother, wife, daughter, sister, friend, graduate student, counselor intern, Brazilian, and immigrant. *Amigas,* we are together for a reason. Let's hold our hands and ***rise together***!

Leticia is a mother, wife, daughter, sister, friend, graduate student, counselor intern, Brazilian, and immigrant. She holds a bachelor's degree in psychology from the University of São Paulo, in Brazil. She is a graduate student at the Professional Counseling Department at Webster University. She is a counselor intern at Monarch Immigrant Services, currently seeing clients at *Casa de Salud*. She loves working with people and helping them with their personal development. She is a former human resources professional, working as a recruiter and talent specialist for international companies. She is from Brazil and began her journey abroad in 2010, traveling to the U.S. and Mexico. She has been in St. Louis since 2018, dedicating her time to family, studying, and welcoming international women through volunteering at the International Mentoring Program. She believes that friendships and connections are empowering tools for life.

Please scan the QR code to connect with this author.

Elsa Ávila

The Hero I Was Waiting For

My Roots

My story begins the day I was born, in Mexico, to a mother who wasn't ready to have me. Her life had been marked by childhood wounds and painful decisions that pushed her away from her role as a mother. Still, I thank her for giving me life. Due to difficult circumstances, she left me in the care of the owner of the business where she worked. The women there took turns watching me, but one woman, the owner, grew deeply attached to me. She had lost her daughter, who was born on the exact same day as I was. Since then, she embraced me as if I were hers. My mother, already separated and struggling financially, accepted her offer to leave me fully in the woman's care.

Later, my Aunt Minerva came into the picture. I don't know exactly when or how, but she gave me a stable life for a while. She couldn't have children and treated me as if I were her own. I have beautiful pictures from that time that include images where I look loved and cared for. Like many stories we cannot control, my mother reappeared one sunny day when I was about two years old. That day changed everything. She took me to live in Michoacán with my grandmother and her children. What seemed like a warm welcome soon turned into a nightmare in disguise.

My mother took me from a safe home only to leave me with a woman who was already overwhelmed, the matriarch of the family. The house was full of uncles, cousins, siblings…and constantly shifting rules. There was no father figure present, no emotional stability, and no safe space. There, I learned I was worthless. I felt I was a burden and that I was not pretty. I had to obey, stay quiet, and survive. They stole my childhood and forced me to grow up too soon.

The Invisible Chains

My grandmother asked me to call her "Mom," so I did. Even though my biological mother was still around, she was sometimes present, but mostly absent. I never really had a father. I was raised calling two women "Mom," and neither of them made me feel whole. At school, I would hear my classmates talk about their parents. I couldn't relate. I would think, "I wish it were my mom or dad hitting me. At least then I'd feel like I belonged to a real family." That deep desire to belong led me, as a young woman, to try to build a family of my own with a man who became my greatest source of pain. He made me feel completely broken. The worst part was watching him repeat that pain with our children when they were just babies. For years, I felt trapped in cycles of abuse and emotional dependence. I was always waiting to be chosen, protected, rescued, but no one came.

The Awakening

One day, I chose to become that person for myself. It wasn't easy. I had to break down everything I believed about love, self-worth, and success. I had to unlearn the idea that I had to earn love, that I had to be "good" to be cared for, that I had to silence myself to be accepted. I rebuilt myself from the ground up.

The Birth of Elsa's Cleaning Company

I moved to the United States with big dreams and strong determination. I didn't have a college degree, and I didn't know how to start a business. I began at the bottom, cleaning houses alone. Step by step, through hard work, discipline, and a clear vision, I turned that small seed into what is now Elsa's Cleaning Company, a thriving business in St. Louis, Missouri. We provide residential and commercial cleaning services, and we create opportunities for others to succeed, lifting them as I climb.

Today, Elsa's Cleaning Company does more than clean; it creates jobs, inspires, educates, and empowers other women to build their own path. I mentor women entrepreneurs, especially immigrant Latinas, who want to start their own cleaning businesses. My motto is simple: *"Either we all grow, or none of us grows."* I deeply believe that knowledge is not meant to be kept; it's meant to be shared. I help others achieve what I've achieved, not from theory, but from lived experience.

My purpose is clear: to show that success is possible. It doesn't matter where you come from, how many times you've fallen, or how often others have made you doubt your worth, you can rise, you can heal, you can shine. And most importantly, you can show your children through your example that there is nothing more powerful than a woman determined to rewrite her story.

Beyond Business

I'm a mother to five incredible children, and they are my biggest motivation. Everything I do is for them. That's why I also prioritize my health: I attend CrossFit classes, maintain healthy habits, and protect my Sundays as sacred time for family lunches and meaningful connections. Balancing business and motherhood is not easy, but I do it with love and purpose. Every decision I make is aligned with the legacy I want to leave.

My children, without knowing it, became my reason to get up, to fight, to start dreaming of a different life. It's a life where love doesn't hurt, a life where they could heal, and I could too. That's where the dream of salvation began. My version of the American Dream was never about money, luxury, or fame. My American Dream was to save us, to save our lives, and to give my children a better life. I came to this country for a life with peace, without screaming, without beatings, without fear. I wasn't running from hunger; I was running from pain. I was searching for something deeper: dignity, love, and safety. This is where I began to find the answers.

I started cleaning houses. In that job, I found more than clients. I found family structures that taught me how life could be. I learned by observing. I saw how other mothers organized their homes, how they treated each other, and how they spoke to their children. That's when I began to rebuild myself. Little by little, I understood that I could offer that to my own children too. I could also create structure, stability, and love. I realized my job wasn't just to clean houses; it was to clean wounds, rebuild broken pieces, and build a new home from the ground up. I validated my children as valuable human beings. I validated myself as a mother, as a woman, as a person. The cleaning business was the vehicle, but the real engine was always them: my children. They were, are, and will always be the reason why I chose to change my story, the reason I chose to rise. Even though the path has been hard, I keep walking with my head held high, because now I know who I am. I know that all this pain was not in vain.

What's Next

My vision goes far beyond business success. I want to create a real impact. I dream of helping children in need and supporting elderly people who are living on the streets. I want to build something bigger than myself. I want to build a network of support, a movement of women who choose themselves, who heal, who build, who lead. Every step I take brings me closer to that vision.

From Victim to Leader

One of the biggest turning points was when I discovered that my pain could be used as fuel. That my voice, which I had learned to silence, could become my most powerful tool. I started speaking, sharing my story, and helping other women, especially immigrant women like me. There are many women who feel lost, who are carrying their own invisible weights. I built a business. I started mentoring. I made a difference, but more importantly, I started believing in myself. Now, when I look in the mirror, I don't see a broken little girl anymore. I see a warrior, a healer, and a leader. Every time I help another woman reclaim her power, I'm reminded:

We're not here to be saved.

We're here to save ourselves.

*Sometimes, the hero you've been waiting for…**is you.***

If you're reading this and you see yourself in any part of my story, I want you to know that "you can rise too." You can heal, grow, start over, find love again, and shine. If you need cleaning services, business support, or simply want to connect, reach out. Together, we can build a better future, one where success is shared and growth belongs to everyone.

Elsa Ávila is the founder of Elsa's Cleaning Company, a mother of five, and a woman who turned pain into purpose.

Her story didn't start with success or opportunity. It started with challenges, deep emotional wounds, and a weight she didn't know how to carry. But it was in the middle of all that chaos that Elsa discovered her true power. Her children became her greatest teachers. Through them, she learned what it means to love without limits, to rise without excuses, and to keep going even when everything inside you wants to give up. Today, she stands as a leader, mentor, and living proof that the very struggles meant to break you can become the foundation for a life you never imagined possible.

Please scan the QR code to connect with this author.

Marissa Southards, MBA

Thriving Through Chaos

If there's one woman reading this who's ever questioned whether she could come back from the chaos, this is for you. I didn't write this to inspire you with a pre-packaged fairytale or to pretend I had it all figured out. I wrote this because I've lived—a lot. I learned it was possible to be seen, even when you feel invisible. Circumstances, no matter how big or painful, how defining they seem to be, don't have the final word. We do. This is a part of my story, but it could just as easily be yours.

I was born in a small town in Ohio with more cornfields than street-lights and a high school that doubled as a tornado shelter. We didn't have much, but my mom kept my brother and me alive with more love than money, and more grit than guidance. Mom did the best she could, raising my brother and I through a variety of odd jobs and two husbands. My dad left early on, chasing musical dreams and a cocaine addiction like they were gospel. He was gone before I even had the language to ask why. My stepdad was a functional alcoholic who believed control came with his fists. My mom convinced herself that a flawed father figure was better than none, although we weren't convinced. She stayed with him for 18 years, until the day came that she decided she didn't need the abuse anymore. We couldn't wait to help her pack his things up.

We moved to St. Louis when my stepdad was transferred here for work. I was entering middle school, which is a tricky transition. As a new kid from "Nowhere," Ohio, who didn't know how to navigate big city middle school politics, this was a recipe for finding myself firmly in the misfit camp. I was the kid who wore knockoff brands with the wrong haircut. I didn't have the confidence to pretend it didn't matter to me either. Not fitting in teaches you skills like how to observe before speaking, how to read the room, how to match conversational cadence, and how to stop caring about being invited into rooms you're not in.

As an adult, the odds weren't stacked in my favor either. There was no roadmap. I had no legacy career waiting for me. There was no generational wealth. Everything I've done was self-created and sometimes stitched together with duct tape and stubbornness. Somewhere between Midwest resilience and a scrappy misfit mindset, I figured out that life doesn't just happen to you. You build it on your terms, even if it's one stubborn, spiteful step at a time. We must intentionally decide to keep going. We give in to the circumstances and the preconceived ideas of who we "should" be, but the longer, bumpier road needs us to be steadfast. I've taken a lot of long roads on purpose, but those roads were still mine. That matters.

One road that I'm still on is the journey of a thousand medical problems. At 19, my body betrayed me. I was diagnosed with polymyositis, an autoimmune disease I hadn't even heard of before it took up residence in every muscle I needed to function. I ended up in Deaconess Hospital for two months and BJC for one, spiraling into multi-organ failure because of a sudden autoimmune response from pneumonia. My body stripped itself down to the basics of survival. Walking, feeding myself, writing my name, dressing myself…all had to be relearned with my care team. My doctors provided the diagnosis, but those nurses and therapists saved my life. After two years of recovery, my body healed as best it could.

Healthcare has a different lens for patients. I saw what it meant to depend on others totally. I also saw where the cracks were. I saw what compassion could do when it showed up in action, and the damage left behind when it didn't. I would build my career trying to undo that damage.

I made my way to nursing school, trying to turn that experience into a way to undo the damage of a world with little compassion. I figured out that bedside care wasn't for me. It wasn't that I wasn't capable of compassion, but it's almost like I cared too much. Around 2004, I found my way into a different side of healthcare, staffing. I was good at observation and reading into the nuance of conversations, so maybe recruiting nurses would be better for me. It was! Staffing felt like the perfect intersection of impact and strategy. I was able to impact entire units of patients and help build better systems. I felt I was undoing a damaged system and changing the world.

I stayed in the industry, and I grew my skills in recruiting and added business development. Through the years, I climbed the corporate ladder as best I could. I earned some promotions and some write-ups for insubordination. I was never built to play at corporate politics, and reaching the C-Suite was something I didn't aspire to. I had found my footing, and I was able to make an impact in the world. I also got married and started a family during this time, so I felt like I had hit a point in my life where I truly had it all. The misfit girl from the South Side had "made it." I was rising!

In 2014, I was forever changed. My life wasn't just shaped by what happened to me up to that point, but also by what I walked toward. Somewhere amid raising children, building a career, and managing a household, *and* autoimmune consequences, I made another choice: to be more than a bystander in the world. Mike Brown was murdered in 2014 in Ferguson, MO, twelve miles from my home. I fully stepped into activism that year. Social justice was human justice. I welcomed the uncomfortable, necessary process of unlearning everything I thought I knew about power structures, privilege, systemic racism, marginalization, and identity. I read books and attended conferences on the school-to-prison pipeline and the new Jim Crow. I showed up to protests and put my body on the line against lines of riot police. I took my fair share of pepper spray and tear gas. What I noticed out there on the front lines is that women showed up. Black women and women of color specifically. They already carried the emotional labor of raising babies, keeping the lights on, getting food on the table, *and* fighting for a society to treat them equally and with equity. They took the most grief from the men around us. Women in general always do anyway.

My introduction to activism wasn't graceful. When I first hit the streets, I forgot to observe and adapt. I forgot to read the room. I had moments where I misspoke. I learned about restorative justice and accountability to those harmed. It was messy, but it gave me something invaluable: a chance to define myself on my own terms and to welcome living in an unapologetic state.

From that growth, The Awakenings Project STL was born as a women's photographic initiative rooted in truth, art, resistance, and healing. My husband taught me how to use a camera, and capturing the first image gave me a place to stand. I could say. "This is who I am, what I care about, and maybe someone else's path won't have to be quite so hard."

I photographed over 400 women and girls from 2015 to 2018, each telling their story, defining themselves in a word of their choice written on their body, and actualizing their truth for the camera. It was tiring, but there's a different kind of exhaustion that comes from caring deeply, publicly, and consistently. There's a different kind of power as you lean into challenging society's ideas and learn to be as loud as you can be. I learned to use my voice not just to tell my story, but to invite others to tell theirs. The women of TAP-STL challenged society's rules, and we challenged ourselves to continue to live in our world. There was joy, sorrow, and lessons throughout the life of the project. I still carry that with me. These lessons are the lessons I pass on to my daughters, the women I mentor through advocacy or activism, and even to my husband. I carried that passion and fire with me into the other parts of my life, too. I earned another bachelor's degree and a master's degree. I entered leadership in my career. Those rooms I was missing out on? They are simply incomplete without me in them.

Then breast cancer came. Hard stop. Screeching brakes. If there was ever a time I wanted to choose the easy path, cancer was it. I wanted to just cave in to the trauma and the surgery, and the tests and poking and prodding and pain. It would have been so easy to just live there in those cancer-ridden weeds, but I didn't. I kept working, even when it meant Zoom calls with a bandaged chest and wound care several times a day. I kept focusing on the bright side and talking up the positive, even while nursing muscle spasms and lymphedema, trying not to cry from the pain. I kept showing up because uplifting others reminded me that I was still alive, even when I felt broken.

Acceptance wasn't pretty. I wasn't some graceful warrior cancer princess from a Lifetime movie. There was no happy ending. I was pissed off. I wanted to scream when people said I was "so strong." I moved forward because I had to, but I was carrying heavy baggage that no one could see. I refused to stop seeing the amazing people around me, though. I never stopped affirming, encouraging, and simply believing in the women in my world. I think that by believing in them, I would find the courage to keep believing in myself, because there were a lot of days this past year that I didn't. A woman I photographed once told me I made her feel like she could take up space in a room that she wasn't supposed to be in. I remembered that after my double mastectomy, and as cliché as it is, that made this whole process seem worth it at that moment. That memory gave me the strength to know that I'm doing the best I can with what I have, and to say, "Today, that's enough." Some days, saying that out loud is the strongest thing I'll do.

Autoimmunity. Cancer. Broken homes. Absentee parents. These are circumstances—things that happen in our lives. Here's the truth: Circumstances won't always be fair to you, but we get to decide who we become in response. I've taken trauma and built purpose. I've lived with pain and created space for others to acknowledge theirs and who they are. I've been absolutely wrecked and still, I survived.

My husband and daughters have watched me break down and rebuild more times than I can count. They've seen me at my weakest, crying over bandages and body parts I no longer have. They have seen that survival isn't something to be ashamed of, and strength doesn't always shout. They're growing up knowing that they don't have to be perfect to be powerful, and that I will lift them and love them no matter what, and that vulnerability is okay. A collective of women formed through the lens of a camera is passing forward those lessons even now, years later, lifting others as they climb.

If I could go back and say anything to the misfit girl who used to observe and adapt and try to assimilate, who used to cry and wonder if she would ever be heard or if she would ever really rise above her circumstances, I'd look at her and say, "You did, sweet girl. You just had to get loud enough to hear yourself." Eleanor Roosevelt said, "Life is what you make of it." Through the chaos of my upbringing, to the circumstances that brought my life to where it is today, I can only say that, yes, Mrs. Roosevelt is right—even if you have to build it out of broken pieces.

Marissa is best known as a snarky realist who spends her days in the healthcare staffing world, and her downtime wondering if she should adopt more dogs, take more pictures, or go for a run.

She is active in her community and professional circles, having served on young professional boards and holding membership in several honor societies for business. She has also been known to participate in civil disobedience from time to time when the situation calls for it.

Outside of the day-to-day, Marissa enjoys a full life with her husband of 20 years, two teen daughters, and two dogs. A resident of St. Louis, MO, she loves running and photography, often combining those passions to capture the beauty of her outdoor adventures in her city.

Please scan the QR code to connect with this author.

Laura Torres

Send the Elevator Down

Declaration and Purpose—Say It Loud, Not *Calladita!*

Stepping into this next chapter of my career, I carry a renewed sense of purpose. *Calladitas Rising* challenged me to reflect, not just on my past, but on the legacy I want to build. This isn't just a reflection; it's a declaration of what I stand for and who I stand with, my *amigas*, my daughters, and every woman who dares to rise.

Being part of *Amigas Rising* is an honor. As a Latina, a mother, a mentor, and a leader, I've learned that success is measured not by how far we go alone, but by how we lift others along the way. I've been guided by a circle of strong women whose quiet strength carried me through. Now, it's my turn. I want my daughters, and my sons, to know that true leadership means building bridges, opening doors, and ensuring no one is left behind. I'm rising because others believed in me. Now I rise so others can too.

A Legacy of Lifting—Let Me Build It!

I come from strong, stubborn, and humble women who taught me: When one rises, we all rise. My mother often told me, "You're allowed to go farther than I did." Her sacrifices became my foundation, and now, my vision for the next generation. There was a time I lost sight of that truth, overwhelmed by life's detours. But my mother's story and those of the women before me never left me. They reminded me who I am and why I'm here.

Amigas Rising is my tribute to them. It's for every woman who leads with *corazón*, breaks ceilings, and clears a path for others. This is the legacy I choose: to rise and lift as I go.

Creating Community and Connection— We're in This Together

Growing up Latina, I learned the power of community through community gatherings, warm hugs, and the quiet understanding that we're in this together. That same spirit followed me to community college, where I became president of the Latino Student Association. I didn't have all the answers, but I knew I wanted students like me to feel seen and supported. That was my first glimpse of real impact. We celebrated our cultures, mentored first-gen students, and raised scholarship funds, not just for tuition, but to say: *You matter. You belong.*

Years later, I met Eliza. We connected by phone about a scholarship for aspiring tax professionals. She reminded me of my early days as a young military spouse; so hopeful, overwhelmed, and determined. After she was accepted, she sent me a thank-you note, sharing how the opportunity would change her life and support her family. I felt a deep responsibility to help her thrive. From that day on, I checked in regularly, shared every opportunity I could, and rooted for her like a big sister. These moments remind me why I do this work. Building connection, creating space, and walking alongside others, that's how we rise. Together.

Mentorship as a Mission—Finding My *Adelita*!

One of the greatest honors of my life has been crossing paths with mentors who, without even realizing it, guided me toward purpose-driven work and helped me reconnect with passions I thought I had lost.

Midway through my life, while trying to reclaim my identity and step beyond the cycles of military life, I discovered the LSLP program. That's where I met Adela. She was the first Latina in years to show up in a space like that, radiating brilliance, insight, and authenticity. Her presence alone reminded me of what was possible. Adela didn't just lead; she inspired. Without knowing it, she mentored me at a time when I needed it most.

Mentorship is one of the most tangible ways we can lift as we climb. It's how we pass on knowledge, open doors, and create ripple effects that extend far beyond what we can see. I remember when Adela first introduced me to the concept of *"sending the elevator down,"* the idea that once you've made it to a certain level, it can be the second floor, the seventh, or the tallest skyscraper, it's your responsibility to go back and lift others up with you. It wasn't just a metaphor to her; I believe it has been her way to lift others.

For someone like me, who had spent years navigating identity, career shifts, and the unique challenges of being a military spouse and a Latina professional, her words hit deep. Adela showed me that success isn't just about climbing higher, it's about making sure the door stays open for those coming behind you. My relationship with Adela reminded me that we don't rise alone. That our achievements mean more when we use them to create space for others, especially those who've been historically left out or overlooked. *"Sending the elevator down"* became more than a phrase; it became a commitment. A call to action.

Since that moment, I've tried to embody that same mindset in how I mentor, in how I network, and in how I speak up in rooms that once felt too big for me. Because if Adela hadn't reached back, I might never have stepped into my own power. Now it's my turn to do the same for others… lead with a purpose. ***Thank you, Adela, for sharing the elevator while we rise with others!***

Leading with Purpose and Compassion— Like a Boss Lady!

Before I got to experience leadership in action, I first had to experience leading with compassion. In this new phase in my life, I grew and reached heights that I never thought I would. I was shown that leadership is about service. It's about using our influence to create space, shift systems, and amplify voices that too often go unheard. It's about making decisions that reflect not just what's good for us, but what's good for others, especially those who've been left out of the conversation, perhaps others like me.

I remember the day I met Denise—wow, what an incredible *Jefa*. She spoke with a strong tone, led meetings with precision, and always got straight to the point. What I loved most as I got to know her was the tough and sincere love, the way she acknowledged my challenges while turning every mistake into a growth opportunity. Because of her leadership and firm kindness, I started to recognize a hidden talent within me that I had long overlooked. And yes, I also became aware of the areas I needed to strengthen in order to rise with intention and clarity.

Bosses like Denise don't just supervise, they invest. They listen, they teach, and they create safe spaces where people feel seen, even in moments of failure. They challenge you because they believe in your potential, not in spite of it. They share work credit, the spotlight, and encourage you to use your voice, even when you're still finding it. Denise showed me that true leaders create pathways, not barriers.

Amigas like Denise remind me that we don't have to choose between strength and softness, vision and vulnerability. The best leaders in my circle of support lead with both. They balance strategy with empathy. They don't hoard opportunity; they multiply it. **Thank you, Boss Lady; your leadership left a mark that continues to shape the way I lead my**

career and try to lift others along the way. Always self-conscious of my personal growth.

Rising Through Adversity—Mom

The path to leadership isn't always straight, and it certainly doesn't start at the top. For me, it began in a small, humble kitchen perhaps, watching my mom lead our family with quiet strength, relentless love, and a kind of wisdom that doesn't come from books, but from life. Leadership looks different in every culture and in every family. And while the world often associates leadership with job titles or boardrooms, I've come to understand it starts much earlier, in much simpler ways. It starts with a woman like my mom, who shows up, over and over again, sometimes with grace, sometimes with stubborn insistence, but always with love.

I've faced plenty of closed doors, quiet dismissals, and hard lessons. But through every setback, my mom has been there. Not always with fanfare or perfect timing; sometimes, her help came wrapped in unsolicited advice or "annoying" interventions that made me roll my eyes, but I always knew the intention was love. Deep, unwavering, *I'll carry this with me*, my mom, my first *amiga* on the rise.

Her support was real, and when I faltered, she reminded me of who I was. When I've been overwhelmed, she's jumped in, sometimes without asking, to shoulder the weight. And now, as she gets older, that same fierce energy still shows up. A little more stubborn, a little more tender, and somehow, even more powerful.

My mom taught me that rising in the face of adversity doesn't mean pretending everything is okay. It means showing up anyway. It means being strong enough to be vulnerable, brave enough to ask for help, and generous enough to offer it, even when your own hands are full. That's the kind of leadership I want my children to see and carry forward: rooted in love, built in kitchens, nurtured in silence, and passed down through generations.

My contribution to *Amigas Rising* honors women like my mom, like my mentors, like the boss ladies in my life; the ones who rise not because it's easy, but because they must. The ones who lift even when their own load is heavy. The ones whose love might come in unexpected forms, yet is always exactly what we need. Because sometimes, the greatest leaders are not the ones who stand in front, but the ones who quietly walk beside us, steady, loving, and always ready to catch us if we fall.

A New Vision for the Future—Nanis + Sami

My daughters, and my future *amigas*, they will grow up with a different vision of leadership. One that doesn't just echo titles or positions, but one that reflects the quiet strength of their grandmother and the hard-earned lessons we've gathered along the way.

Together, we are building the ladders, the stairways, reaching the elevators that we use, not just to rise, but to carry others with us. I want them to see leadership as something rooted in compassion, collaboration, and courage. I want them to recognize that lifting others isn't a burden, it's a privilege and a responsibility.

I'm working hard to reclaim and redefine leadership for them, one that makes room for grace, truth, and equity. A leadership that shows up with intention and heart. One that says: "*I see you. I believe in you. Let me make space for you.*" My mother and the women of her generation may not have had the chance to lead in visible ways, but they led through action, through sacrifice, and through unwavering care. Their strength built the foundation I now stand on, and my daughters will rise because of that legacy.

As I write this, I imagine the day Nanis and Sami will read these words. I hope they'll feel proud, not just of me, but of the women who came before them. I hope they'll feel empowered to speak up, take space, and build bridges. I hope they'll carry this spirit into classrooms, boardrooms, and every space they occupy, rising boldly and reaching back, just as generations of women have done for them.

To my sons, I hope they, too, are shaped by this vision. That they grow to be kind, thoughtful leaders who uplift the *amigas* and daughters in their lives, who champion equity, and who understand that true strength lies in empathy, respect, and shared purpose. Because rising through adversity doesn't stop with us, it plants seeds for the future. And my greatest hope is that all my children grow into leaders who know: They were never meant to rise alone.

Together, We Rise. I Am Rising!

This is my story, but it's also *our story*. This is a story of *amigas* who lift, lead, love deeply, and act bravely. It's a story that belongs to every woman who's ever said, "Come with me," instead of "Look at me." It's a story I will keep telling, writing, and living, for my daughters, your daughters, and every future leader still finding their voice.

Together, we rise.

Together, we build.

Together, we lead with love.

Amigas, together for life!

Laura Torres is the director of workforce innovation programs for a recognized nonprofit. She supports military-connected career initiatives and program outreach. A recent contributor to the *Calladitas Rising* anthology, she joins this *Amigas Rising* anthology with meaningful thoughts and stories of mentorship and support that have allowed her to *rise* in her own career growth. She recently created Latinas Leading Northwest, where she is creating a safe space for Latinas in the Northwest region to meet, grow, and connect. She also became part of the Oregon Small Business Development Center in the Eastern region, where she advises small businesses.

Laura earned a bachelor of arts in liberal studies with a concentration in early childhood education and an MBA with a concentration in human resource management. After relocating to California, Laura had to retrain in a new career to advance in a competitive community.

She volunteers for service veteran organizations and supports local civilian organizations. As a military caregiver, she enjoys life with her retired veteran husband, who served in the Marine Corps for 21 years. They have four beautiful grown children and enjoy Pacific Northwest life.

Please scan the QR code to connect with this author.

Lizett Mata

Gift from God

"Long live Mexico! Long live the Virgin of Guadalupe!" This phrase has resonated in my heart since I was little and long before I became an executive business professional, community leader, and artistic director. In my family, giving thanks and giving blessings to others was a positive way to instill, without knowing it, faith in myself, in others, and in the Holy Trinity.

Growing up uplifted me, built endurance, and imparted to me fortitude to overcome every challenge. I remember walking to the plaza to participate in Sunday Mass, festivals, and fireworks after the religious celebrations. In that same parish church, I would pass long hours of silence in prayer with the Blessed Sacrament and adore the Holy Cross during Holy Week. I vividly remember during the festivities of Lady of Guadalupe at Christmas, the colorful lights, *piñatas*, and crafts. I remember my aunts talking about the great miracles they wanted to happen. I understood the party very well, but not what miracles were. It took me more than 30 years to understand the true meaning of prayer and miracles. At the age of nine, I lost my father, and I heard my mother say: *You are a beautiful gift from God.* Then, I had the impulse to go to the temple like my aunts and my mother to raise my requests to heaven. Inside a girl's head, it is difficult to understand death.

My magical hometown of Guanajuato, Mexico, was a 1500s Spanish colony founded on wealth and tradition, where baroque temples and mining life predominated. This is where a woman dedicated herself exclusively and diligently to the care of the house and the family. There, I graduated with a degree in international trade from the University of Guanajuato. This inspired my interest in culture and religious affairs, in addition to my studies. Foreigners from all countries would arrive in my state to pursue university and postgraduate studies. Many of those visitors did not understand the traditions of our cultural or religious calendar. My childhood faith weakened upon this encounter with new and different beliefs. The importance of thinking positively and having faith in blessings, coming from my religious and cultural tradition, has been a part of my life. My catechesis was poor and basic, but filled with the love of God and community.

The concept of blessing and asking God to fill us with his providence and mercy prevailed in my heart. After losing my father, I prayed for my mother, for my siblings, and for our well-being. We never went without food, but there was deprivation. In the family, we didn't talk openly about vices. These vices are the same in many cultures. The dark experiences remain in the silence of the community.

Faith and Love—Where It Began and How It Grew

My life changed forever when, after a car accident and three months of convalescence, my father died. My mother became the leader of the household, not seeing herself having a bright future. Amazingly, she was not afraid. She said, "We are going to move forward." She was the first person in my life to teach me collaboration and faith in action. She didn't spend her time in the temple like my aunts, but she had faith in herself and God. I learned to see her love for her three children while she was putting aside her dreams as a sacrifice for us. Margarita's love and dedication were unlimited for us, unstoppable, and unmatched, always lifting us up. She started a business selling on the street. I learned business skills by watching her. She was patient and cheerful at negotiating, in marketing her products, and excelled in administration. She was, above all, passionate, dedicated, and strong. I learned all of that from her. She was a demonstration of faith lived out in action. This role for women was not very traditional. She never remarried. She often said, "I live to give a profession to my three children, a university degree." I think she gave us more than that! It was proclaimed, and so it happened.

At fifteen years old, I came to her with my dream of being a dancer. She paused, and didn't say "No" at first. She tried to be as positive as she could to not crush my dream. She understood the real desire to do something meaningful. She asked me to talk to my grandfather and get good advice. He was a revolutionary man who lived during the Cristero War in central Mexico. I thought he was going to discourage me, but it was the opposite! He told me to dance for his 80th birthday. I began to plan the choreographies, the music, the dancers, the costumes, and the stage. He told me after finishing, "You are an artistic director, God's dancing gift." My mom, as a good collaborator, sought help and other mentors for me. I learned that seeking help and good counsel was very important for the well-being and triumph of life. They did not try to solve the problem by imposing, but by encouraging. Both knew the path of encouragement to have better opportunities. By then, I was a teenager, enterprising and diligent; they knew that imposition was not going to work on me.

Perhaps this was the opportunity that my mother herself would have wanted to receive from her mining father. Instead of studying, she proudly raised three children with limited resources, which ironically turned out to be the occasion for my family's miracle of perseverance and self-determination! She stood out and always sought self-improvement, proudly allowing me to graduate with a business degree.

Mentors—How Strong Mentors Impacted My Life

After college, I immigrated to California, leaving behind my culture and tradition. Suddenly, I turned into a cosmopolitan woman. Thanks to my grandfather's good advice, my dream of being a professional dancer did not vanish. It was on hold while I focused on being a successful business professional. The first barrier was to understand another culture, another language, and another people. I remembered the students who arrived in Guanajuato and who were in the same shoes, having immigrated to another country. It was another new beginning; however, my case was different. From the beginning, I had the support and encouragement of my husband. Then, a married couple allowed me to take care of their daughters. The wife was my first professional leader and mentor. She saw in me the potential that I would never have imagined. She was a psychologist who was preparing to receive her PhD from the University of California. She encouraged me to continue studying English as a second language and to pursue my dream as a dancer. My dream of being a dancer came true, along with the most honorable job of being a mother. Soon after, I moved to the Bay Area, where for ten years I had a fast-track professional career. This secured my role as a manager with the best coaching as I moved up the corporate ladder. Relocating to St. Louis as a manager would change my life forever.

Intercession for Others

Thirteen years after leaving my hometown, my mother, Margarita, had to undergo surgery, and the doctor gave her no hope. My siblings asked me to come to her rescue, and I did. After many years of being separated, my mom and I met again. During that time, I understood the power of helping one another, just as I had experienced when I first began living in a foreign country. A few women offered me their help. My aunt and Godmother came to my aid. She always told me, "God has given us the free will to choose." She was a manager of a prestigious company and traveled extensively as a missionary, helping indigenous communities in Mexico. She helped me to see religion in a different way. She saw it as a vocation of faith in our lives, always helping others and sharing all one's gifts, uplifting others with the power of the Holy Spirit. At this very moment, I could use such a gift! She was a part of bringing a miracle into my life. She prayed for me to become a "gift from God." She and my other aunties had been precisely that for me: a gift from God, a blessing. Her presence reminded me of my identity and many treasured memories. All of this came together in my heart, working together as an inspiration.

Gift from God

May you never forget that God loves you personally. May He inflame your heart with a passion as you serve others, especially those who are lonely, troubled, and need someone who will listen. While my mother was convalescing, I could feel the presence of the Holy Spirit, and this deepened my sense of identity as a daughter of God. I remember vividly my mother's prayers, her blessings, her desire for a miracle. In that challenging time of suffering together with my mother, I remembered my father again. More than ever, I wanted a miracle. I knew that if my mom died, I wouldn't see her again.

Before, my only desire was to be a successful professional and dancer. After my mom's health issues, I began the habit of powerful prayer, asking for miracles to achieve complete happiness. I was thirty-three and a successful professional woman. Now, I received another call: to be a woman of faith and to raise petitions to heaven. This was the beginning of a new reality for my faith and a deeper encounter with Jesus. This testing of my priorities upon witnessing the delicate balance between life and death for my best friend, my mother—I call this "divine justice." I remembered what a miracle of faith was. My life, my desire, became wanting to be close again to that woman who gave everything for me and inspired me to become a *gift from God*. Yes, there was a lot to think about. As I walked to the plaza of my hometown square, I recognized that I needed a miracle. When I returned home, I saw a bookcase full of books that my mother was studying. To my surprise, that woman wanted to improve and learn. In the bookcase was a book called *My First Prayers*. I took it and I began to ask the Virgin of Guadalupe, the Virgin Mary, "*La Morenita*," to please bless my mother. I remembered how Mary, the mother of Jesus, was at the foot of the cross when her lovely Son was about to be crucified. I raised my hands to heaven and offered Mary my request to intercede with Jesus to save my mother. The image I will never forget was me in this moment offering up a prayer of surrender. I asked Mary to intercede with Jesus to give me more time with my mother. When the Feast of the Virgin of Guadalupe came around, I went to the temple, and I asked her for a miracle. In exchange, I would offer my service to the church. Mary, a woman, changed the course of my life. After that miracle, my mom has been with me until now. I know it will be until eternity by prayer, just like with all the people I've related to and with whom I have become a *gift from God*.

My destiny changed from an international business executive to a missionary of the faith. I thank God for twenty-seven years of professional success, lifting others along the way. Now that I have been called to this walk of faith, I ask for grace and blessing for another miracle so that I may continue to raise my hands to heaven in thanksgiving, praise, and petition for others. I want to be able to continue to inspire the tradition of praying and blessing every woman in my life, reminding them *they are a beautiful gift from God*. Long live the Virgin of Guadalupe!

Lizett Mata is a motivated, gifted, self-driven person. She is a native Mexican-American, holds a BA in International Trade, is a professional, community leader, dancer, prayer warrior, and an artistic director. She devoted twenty-seven years to corporate international business affairs, working for the top five hundred companies with increasing responsibility until being promoted to director and compliance officer.

Today, Lizett is dedicated to uplifting the St. Louis community around prayer and formation in the Catholic Faith at the Charismatic Renewal Center, using her managerial, administrative, and executive leadership skills to put faith in action. Her joy and passion as a dancer inspired her to create *BailaMe* Academy, which specializes in Mexican Folklore Heritage, Art, and Tradition (HAT) to build trust and uplift all generations to pursue their dance dreams.

Lizett is trained in ballroom, ballet, contemporary, and *flamenco* dance. She was a YMCA-awarded businesswoman in 2018 and is certified in Faith Formation and as a Catechetical leader by the Archdiocese of St. Louis.

Please scan the QR code to connect with this author.

Heather Moss

Stepping Into the Void

I used to be somebody. I was a deputy director, then a director, then a deputy secretary, and again a director. I spent the last 20 years of my professional life as a leader in state, county, and nonprofit organizations ranging in size from 25 to 2500 staff. I had authority. People listened to what I had to say. Then, five and a half years into my most recent appointment as the director of our county social services agency, the newly elected executive told me he was "going in a different direction" and my employment would end in thirty days. Friends and colleagues were quick to tell me I wasn't being fired and that elected officials often make changes to their cabinet when they take office—no big deal. Six months into my premature retirement, though, it still feels like a big deal. Although I'm over the embarrassment of such an abrupt end to my nearly 30-year career in government and social services, I'm still working out what my next steps should be. This is where my chapter begins…reflections on how I've been helped by (and hopefully helped) other women in my life. *Amigas,* I need help rising again!

I'm taking the newly-elected executive's comment to heart—"going in a new direction" is what I need to do, too. After almost 25 years in government and another four in nonprofit leadership, it's time for me to chart a new course, do something different, start fresh…to step into the void. This is not the first time I've stepped into the void. Indeed, that phrase has

defined many of the major milestones in my life, personally and professionally. Looking back, all those steps have been inspired, supported, and
celebrated by amazing women.

I am sure my early bravery came from my parents, Tom and Lynda.
They convinced me I could do anything. What a gift! My first step into
the void took me to Caracas, Venezuela, as a 16-year-old exchange
student. I lived for a year with an amazing Venezuelan family, led by my
host mother, Helena. *Mamá* Helena was a force of nature. She was a mom
of five adult children, a college professor, and a loving spouse. She spoke
three languages, loved to dance, and didn't take any grief. *Mamá* Helena
showed me how to live boldly and not shy away from trying new things,
even when they were scary and I might fail (*¡Bailando salsa! ¡Cuba libres!
¡Empanadas de tiburón! ¡Conversando en Español!*).

Fast forward a decade to another time I stepped into the void, although
this time I had little choice. Three years after marrying my college sweet-
heart, Scott, I became pregnant. At my first check-in with my doctor, at
about 16 weeks, she told me I was "growing rapidly." Since I've always
been an enthusiastic eater, that didn't seem like a big deal to me. Once she
started up the ultrasound machine, though, and swept that wand across
my belly, she confirmed her suspicions—we were having twins. My sons,
Dylan and Dustin (who are now 29), are wonderful people, and I am so
proud of them. Those first weeks, months, even years, though, that was
tough. Thankfully, I had other moms (some also with twins) to help advise
and reassure me, and to laugh with me when it all seemed like too much.
Jill, whose sons Jared and Matt are just a few months older than my boys,
is a friend to this day. She's an amazing architect and wonderful cook, and
I am so grateful we had each other to lean on when our boys were little.
Can you imagine four toddler boys on a "hike?" I was also friends with a
few moms from the YMCA swimming class, but I don't remember their

names. What I do remember is a few child-free nights drinking Cosmo-politans and laughing a lot. Thank goodness for other moms.

As my sons grew older, I started to think about how my professional career should grow and evolve. I worked part-time for a state agency thirty miles from home and was ready for a change. Just then, another amazing woman came into my life. Elizabeth, another mom from my sons' elementary school, asked me to be her deputy director at a state-wide nonprofit agency she had founded a decade earlier. I was flattered, and she was certain. Together, we led the agency for five years, and it was awesome. I would not have thought I was ready for such an important job, but Elizabeth saw something in me that I couldn't see in myself. I'm grateful for and humbled by the opportunity she gave me; it really started me in my executive career.

As I shared earlier, my most recent position was leading the social services agency of our local county government. Working in a male-dom-inated, somewhat conservative local government was a new and chal-lenging environment for me. What made it manageable, though, were my female colleagues. I learned early in my career that you need to always have a handful of peers you can lean on when times are tough, so I created a tight circle of five women leading county agencies, and we got together at least monthly. This band of colleagues (Jody, Betty, Constance, Karen, and Jen) helped me brainstorm problems, listened to my worries, and celebrated my successes. Together, we led our departments through the pandemic, and I know the citizens of our county were better off because of that group of women.

Which brings me to today, but also takes me back to the beginning. I started this chapter by noting how my parents raised me to believe I could do anything I set my mind to. That frame of mind certainly played a part in all the adventures and challenges I described here, and plenty of others. Although my father was taken from us suddenly and too soon (I was just

32 when he died in a car accident; he was only 52 himself), his belief in me continues to carry me to this day. And my mom, well, she's never stopped being my ultimate role model. As a 72-year-old widow, Lynda, who never liked me calling her "Mom," decided she had one more adventure in her life, so she sold the home she'd lived in for 40 years, moved across the country, and started a whole new life in Oregon. After earning her PhD in fine arts in the 80s, when my brother and I were just children, she finally began pursuing a full-time career as an artist. I could write a whole book about Lynda's life and accomplishments. I'm so proud of her!

I share all of this both as a reminder to myself as I embark on this next adventure in life, and also as an inspiration for you. I've been encouraged, boosted, celebrated, and cared for by so many women—friends, family, coworkers—in my life, so I hope to share the same with others. Here's what I've learned from the steps I've taken and the women who inspired them:

It's never wrong to be bold, even if you fail. *Mamá* Helena taught me that doing things that scare you gets you to the good stuff in life.

Lean on your people when you need help or encouragement. As a young mother, I needed those other moms to complain to, learn from, and laugh with.

People come and go from your life for a reason; that's OK. Although I don't remember the swim moms, and I haven't seen my county colleagues in many months, I had real and deep relationships with these women when we needed each other. Some people come into your life and quickly go; others stay for a long time.

Never lose your humility. If you pay attention, you can see there are others around you who will be your champions. Don't be afraid to be vulnerable, because if they are paying attention, the people around you will see your greatness and help lift you up!

It's never too late to keep stepping into the void. Whether it's starting a new stage of life, like Lynda, or trying your hand at a new career, like me, it is never too late to take that next step into the unknown.

I'm ready to rise again, *amigas*. I hope you are, too!

Heather lives in Tacoma, Washington, with her husband of 33 years, Scott. Their favorite pastimes include hiking and traveling with their adult twin sons, Dylan and Dustin. Heather and her family have traveled all over the United States and in Central and South America, supporting a love of exploring new places, eating good food, and speaking Spanish!

Heather has a master's in public administration from the University of Washington and studied at the *Universidad Nacional* in Costa Rica. Having recently completed a successful 30-year career in state and local government and nonprofit leadership, Heather is now considering her next professional move, which will likely include editing, consulting, and coaching.

Please scan the QR code to connect with this author.

Brittany Corners

From Chaos to Community:
The Journey of Progress Over Perfection

One day or day one—that's where my life decided to shift.

For over two decades, I sat at executive tables, often one of the only women, striving to prove I belonged. On the surface, my life looked polished: executive marketer, high-performing, deadline-driven. Beneath the polish, fulfillment was missing. I loved marketing, but I was drawn to something beyond the workplace, somewhere without a glass ceiling. I was running on caffeine and autopilot. My calendar was packed, but my heart was tired. I'd checked every box except the one that asked, "What do you actually want?" I shifted the question from "What do I need to do?" to "Who do I want to be?"

In 2018, I made a choice just for me: I became a certified yoga teacher. It was one of those rare, singular moments you hold your breath through, powerful and quietly seismic. It helped me remember who I truly was and invited me back into my own potential, not just through self-discovery, but through shared intention and the light of a brilliant, caring circle of women. That summer, something quietly and fiercely ignited within me.

Then, serendipity arrived as if in soft focus. Therese, co-owner of the struggling studio where I trained, called me on a cold winter evening and asked if I would join her in owning the studio. Saying "yes" changed everything. I didn't yet know I was inviting in a best friend who would hold both my shadows and my brightest moments or a business partner I never realized I needed. That single "yes" charted a new course for both of our lives.

In 2019, we bought an old house together. With love-drenched sweat from our husbands, family, and friends, it became Moonbird Yoga. What began as a side project became the mirror I didn't know I was looking for, reflecting, reshaping, and lighting me up.

The name *Moonbird Yoga* carries deep significance. A moonbird, a type of godwit, travels unimaginable distances, baffling researchers who thought it had vanished. It hadn't. It was quietly doing the impossible, persevering through storms, a powerful metaphor for our community and our journey.

We juggled schedules, shifts, pivots, staff, events, and admin. After opening just 17 days before being forced to shut down, cracks began to appear. But instead of collapsing, something clicked. I began to see my patterns with clarity: The chaos wasn't new; it was finally undeniable.

When the world shut down in 2020, our newly rebranded studio closed too. Within 24 hours, we pivoted to virtual classes. It was challenging, yes, and awakening. In that stillness, I received a diagnosis I never expected but always needed: ADHD.

What once felt like forgetfulness, distraction, over-talking, or disorganization became my map. ADHD wasn't a limitation; it was my unique wiring—my superpower. The reason I could connect dots others couldn't see, lead with energy, pivot with grace, and build community from chaos.

This shift from shame to self-trust transformed everything, not just for me, but for everyone around me. Success in business and life isn't about fitting a mold; it's about discovering what fuels us and honoring that fire. We stopped chasing perfection and began celebrating progress because this is not a race; it's a marathon.

During this calm-yet-chaotic time, I felt a magnetic pull to align my passion for marketing with my love for yoga. As I began exploring roles in health and wellness marketing, everything lit up. I found a role aligned with my purpose and dove in energized, confident, and ready to use my ADHD as a superpower. Soon, I was leading meditations before team meetings and loving it.

When we reopened the studio, it became more than walls; it became a sanctuary. The women who walked through our doors weren't just clients; they were collaborators, healers, soulmates. We built something that transcended business models. We followed our instincts, trusted the process, and supported each other not performatively, but with real, messy, heart-centered commitment.

Moonbird Yoga has evolved into much more than a studio. It's a place where women can return to themselves. In 2024, we opened a second location, and a third is on the way. It's never been about empire building; it's about energy, community, and empowering women to lead without losing themselves.

I've learned that purpose doesn't always come with a plan. Sometimes it arrives in the form of exhaustion, a whisper, or a friend saying, "I see more in you."

When I stopped trying to force things, the universe met me halfway. I began noticing synchronicities: people arriving at just the right time, partnerships forming effortlessly, ideas flowing when I let go of control. That's the power of surrender. That's the magic of *we*.

I believe we are here to build bridges, not climb ladders. Community is our compass; competition loses meaning when we collaborate.

Our next mission is our boldest yet: transforming a historic church into its own sanctuary—a collective for women in wellness and healthcare to rise together. A place of healing, creativity, and aligned energy. A reminder that we don't have to do it all, we just have to do it together.

To every woman reading this who wonders if it's too late, too messy, or too much, I promise you it's not. Start small. One hour a week. One breath. One truth. One aligned yes. There's no perfect path, only your path, and you never walk it alone.

Brittany Corners is a visionary marketing executive, two-time 500-hour certified yoga teacher, Reiki master, and co-owner of Moonbird Yoga. She balances a thriving corporate role as vice president of marketing at a national health and wellness company while leading three community-centered yoga studios.

Diagnosed with ADHD during the pandemic, Brittany transformed what once felt like chaos into her creative edge. She believes that entrepreneurship and executive leadership don't have to exist in separate worlds; true alignment lives in the "and." Whether in the boardroom or on the mat, she leads with empathy, honesty, and an unwavering belief that community is our greatest compass. Her mission is to help women trust their timing, own their brilliance, and rise together.

Please scan the QR code to connect with this author.

Alexis King

Safe Sharing Heals

I was shocked, numb, scared, and anxious after September 11. One by one, over and over again, I watched the Twin Towers fall. Then I grabbed my uniform out of the truck, determined to be a part of something more meaningful and daunting than cleaning pigeon poop from our supply warehouse at Langley Air Force Base. I canceled the plans my boyfriend and I had to go to an Aerosmith concert that day. Calling my veteran Dad, I was looking for guidance, but there were no words of comfort or sage advice. I sought God as I walked to the ocean, looking for deeper meaning in the midst of tragedy. Then I immediately began pushing people out the door to deploy and watch them respond with valor to the egregious terrorist attacks on the World Trade Center, the Pentagon, and Flight 93.

It was the fear of people willing to kill us that made strangers pause to look each other in the eye, searching for connection, for what was real, and to sense a shared humanity. It was a palpable shock that happened to us all that changed the trajectory of our military from training for war to fighting the global war on terror. It changed traffic patterns and the way we would prepare to fly somewhere with tightened security. It was the beginning of a two-decade fight against terror to protect our nation, its people, and our way of life.

Shortly thereafter, I flew to a training course. Waiting on a flight, I remember sitting at a table waiting with six other strangers. I overheard a man share with these strangers his formula for a new aftershave he was planning to patent and sell. Would the men have sat there talking to each other before September 11?

I stayed anxious. We lived a short drive from D.C., where the terror seemed to continue. I ran and went to church to deal with my stress. There were reports of a sniper who was shooting at people randomly, which added to the stress, leading to our misperception that we were caught in the crossfire. Shortly thereafter, I felt relieved that the sniper was caught. His name fails me, but the feeling of threat and worry is embedded deep in my memory. This led up to the two decades of war fighting for our military and their families.

Three months after my marriage to my husband, I got devastating news from my mom: She had been diagnosed with stage IIIB/IV lung cancer. I collapsed into the chair, wailing at this heart-wrenching news. My mom and I had a rocky relationship as a teenager, but she was the only mom I had. I had lost contact with my dad when I was eleven months old, and he died when I was four. I stood facing the thought of losing my mom and being orphaned just as my life as a mature young adult was beginning.

Three months later, I was scheduled to deploy for the Air Force. How could I possibly leave my dying mother behind? I remember sitting in my Chief's office one day, detailing my dilemma. I told him, "Chief, I don't want to come home to a dead mom." He was kind and had a wife going through cancer treatment. He asked me if I wanted him to talk to the Commander, so I could stay home and care for my mom. I remember thanking him for the gesture and sharing that I felt I had a duty to deploy, since I took the commissioning oath as an officer for the United States Air Force. This was my most patriotic moment, as I had first enlisted so I could one day go to college. Leaving my Chief's office and slumping down at my desk with a feeling of defeat, I stared in front of me at a postcard with an empty chair sitting on the beach facing the ocean. It read: "Be still and know that I am God" (Psalm 46:10). This verse gave me the peace that I needed to deploy and the hope that I would not come home to my biggest fear: a dead mother. We were in God's hands, and I took great comfort from that.

Thanks be to God; I had a great deployment! Sent by my Major as the only female lead of a 12-person advanced (ADVON) team, my team worked hard to set up a bare base in a neighboring country to Iraq, with me serving as the acting Logistics Squadron Commander for the beginning of the war with Iraq. I thank God for my subject matter experts—the superintendents of each logistics career field (supply, transportation, logistics plans, and fuels) who helped ramp up the bare base from 0-7,000 people in 30 days. We helped bed down two aircraft frames and 10 guard units and 6,200 people that joined the 800+ Airmen from our base in the fight against Saddam Hussein and his military. I was blessed with a great Wing Commander, amazing Superintendents, and a great Wingman, who were committed to lifting me up. When we first got there, living for what would be 50 days on Meals-Ready-to-Eat (MREs), we all stood around a bonfire talking about what restaurant we would eat at when we returned home. After weeks of no communication except for duty-related satellite phone usage, I was able to be in touch with my mother and husband via email. It was a blessing to have connectivity and small reminders from home.

With internet access, I remember seeing the names of the patriots who gave their lives for our country being posted online. A deep sadness hit me seeing the names of those who paid the ultimate price, having sacrificed their all on behalf of their families and ours, and I began printing an updated Honor Roll every day in their honor and posted it for all to see. I felt like I was serving a greater cause. While I would have rather been home, I was grateful for this opportunity to serve my country, having immigrated to it at eleven months.

My only regret was not knowing what to do when the tears started flowing for one of my troops when the stress of war and being away from family got to be too much. I wish I knew what I know now. Tears are a natural release to help us process grief, stress, and even joy. If you are reading this, know that I am deeply sorry for not stopping to listen to what you were feeling!

Hindsight, emotional intelligence training, and two decades later, I now realize I was emotionally unavailable to my troop because I had not been permitted to express my feelings as a child. I know how healing crying can be, and I make myself watch a sad movie to get the tears to flow, but I will always tell people they have a safe space to cry with me. I still have guilt and regret for that moment, but in spite of myself, God called me to serve as a chaplain as I helped an Airman in crisis during that deployment. Staying with the member until I got help, our First Sergeant was a blessing in that pivotal time. I am grateful for the chaplains who helped me when I received a call from the Red Cross that my mother's chemo treatment had stopped working. I'll never forget the Wing Commander finding me in the field mess hall and sitting down with me, saying that perhaps now is the time for me to go home to be with my mom. I was grateful for that permission! God had sustained my mom and me, and while I hadn't gone to worship due to work and the distance between the worship tent and my office, the Holy Spirit filled me with faith and renewed it daily through my reading of Psalm 23. Scripture and prayer were a source of comfort for me in a land far away from home in a war zone.

By the grace of God, I survived that wartime deployment and made it home to my dying mother while she was still alive! We were blessed to relocate our jobs to an Air Force Base near her and take care of her in her dying days that summer and fall. It was awful to watch her suffer, but God blessed us with a supportive church! We had an excellent pastoral staff ministering to us with presence, lay ministers who visited her, cooked meals for us, and gave us respite once she needed 24-hour care in the last month of her life.

Not only was I devastated about my mom's decline, but the deployment experience had exhausted me beyond measure, and I had no time to unpack my deployment bags. I never ended up unpacking those bags, symbolizing my desire not to have to deal with that stuff ever again. I was, however, confronted with the problem that arose and conflicted with my conscience: I was excited and happy to go to war to do my part for our country's protection and our freedom in the pursuit of life, liberty, and justice for all people.

We went under the pretense that this was a just war. The intelligence told us the country had weapons of mass destruction. We were going over there for that reason. Then we found out there were no weapons of mass destruction, and I was so conflicted that I did not know what to do with that. I was angry that we were sent over on false pretenses. I was angry at our president, at our Congress, and at the fact that we were following what we thought were lawful orders. Thinking about this as I write this, at the time, those were lawful orders, because we had been told there were weapons of mass destruction in Iraq. However, my conscience was burdened that I had helped start a war and supported a war that was started with misinformation. What was I supposed to do with that? I didn't know, but it burdened me for 20 years until God connected me with the Air Force Chaplain Corps College again for training. Through Chaplain Lumpkin, I learned about the concept of *moral injury*. Studying his doctoral work, I felt a burden had been lifted! I finally had vocabulary for what it was that I had experienced with my involvement with OPERATION IRAQI FREEDOM. I realized I had moral injury once we found out there were no weapons of mass destruction.

Having vocabulary for my symptoms and the cause of them was so liberating. It was like an albatross had been lifted off my shoulders, and I began to study moral injury feverishly so I could educate more veterans and civilians on this concept. I wanted to lift others as I rose from this moral injury.

In this broken world, anyone can experience a moral injury. The study on moral injury is only about 30 years old, even though it has been going on since God created the world. My faith helps me heal from moral injury as I confront it at my own pace, only when I am ready to remember and confront it. Not everyone will incur moral injury. Two people can have the same experience and process it differently (Koenig, 2023).* Studies have shown that members with adverse childhood experiences (ACEs) are more susceptible to moral injury (Dune 2024).* There are experts who have been studying moral injury, and I am grateful to them and my colleague who has contributed to this field in light of military service.* Studies show that if you have PTSD and moral injury, you need to treat each or risk not healing fully from PTSD (Koenig, Carey, and Wortham 2023). I find it of utmost value to our healing journey to learn what moral injury is and to gather with a peer support group to share in a safe space and to be able to process and begin our healing journey. *Safe sharing heals.*

You may ask what moral injury is. Moral injury can be defined as "the enduring consequences of transgressing deeply held moral beliefs and expectations" (Lumpkin 2019).

Moral injury can develop from something you have done, something you have witnessed or heard about, something you failed to prevent, or a betrayal of some sort; betrayal done to you or you betraying someone or your own conscience (Litz et al. 2009).

Moral injury occurs when a morally injurious event or act (you or that of another person or institution or system) goes against your firmly held beliefs or values (conscience) from which various spiritual, emotional, behavioral, social, and/or physical symptoms, including but not limited to, can occur (Litz et al. 2019): guilt, shame, loss of meaning, self-condemnation, difficulty forgiving self or others, spiritual or religious struggles, social withdrawal, aggression, depression, anxiety, excessive alcohol or drug use, inability to sleep, fatigue, memory trouble, grief, feeling numb, lack of self-care, risk of suicide, relationship issues, and quality of sleep (Lumpkin 2017, p. 91).

Moral injury is a wound of the soul or conscience, so consulting a spiritual or religious leader you trust, or a chaplain, can start your healing journey. Connecting with the community is also vitally important. Going alone is not the path to healing, but it can be dangerous and unsafe. You are not alone. You are loved and worthy of healing and a good life! *Safe sharing heals*. God bless you with healing, renewal, restoration, and peace.

Citations:

Dune, Shanta R. *"ACES."* Paper presented at the Comprehensive Moral Injury Conference, Moral Injury Support Network for Servicewomen, Inc. (MISNS). https://misns.org.

Koenig, Harold G., Lindsay B. Carey, and James S. Wortham. *Moral Injury: A Handbook for Military Chaplains.* New York: Amazon Books, 2023. https://www.amazon.com/Moral-Injury-Handbook-Military-Chaplains/dp/B0BRJK1PVB.

Litz, Brett T., Nathan Stein, Eileen Delaney, Leslie Lebowitz, William P. Nash, Caroline Silva, and Shira Maguen. "Moral Injury and Moral Repair in War Veterans: A Preliminary Model and Intervention Strategy." *Clinical Psychology Review* 29, no. 8 (2009): 695–706. https://doi.org/10.1016/j.cpr.2009.07.003.

Lumpkin, Douglas E. *"What Is Moral Injury – 30K View, Moral Injury, eady to Return."* PowerPoint presentation, 2019. ttps://air-af.academia.edu/DouglasLumpkin.

Lumpkin, Douglas E. *Warrior Support Groups: Reducing Moral Injury and Trauma-Related Symptoms through Group Learning.* Doctor of Ministry diss., 2017. https://doi.org/10.13140/RG.2.2.36724.63366.

Alexis King is an ordained minister in the Evangelical Lutheran Church in America (ELCA), serving as a chaplain in the Air Force Reserve and chaplain resident for the VA in St. Louis, MO. Her story does not represent the Department of Defense or the U.S. government. She has served as visitation pastor, interim pastor, chaplain of a continuous care retirement community, supply pastor, and director of children's ministries. An Army brat, she is a prior enlisted, serving in the United States Air Force since 1994. On a Scholarship for Outstanding Airmen through ROTC, she majored in communication and culture at the University of Indiana, receiving her B.A. and first commission to serve in the United States Air Force as a logistics planner. She received her master's in Divinity from Union Presbyterian Seminary in Richmond, VA, in 2009. She is a mom of God-given twins and a lover of God's creation, art, and travel.

Please scan the QR code to connect with this author.

Jackie Duty

The Sherpa Way:
Leading Others to Their Summit

"You can't climb a smooth mountain."
— Zig Ziglar

Every breath was a struggle as the altitude changed. With calluses building, she reached for the next crevice in the side of the mountain, while looking up at the seemingly never-ending wall that reached into the heavens. After hours, days, months, and years, putting her life on the line, she reached the top of the mountain. She paused only for a moment to take in the incredible views while she took a deep breath. The shift in the altitude reminded her that the air was thinner and harder to breathe, but this was a subtle reminder to appreciate every second. Every breath in our lungs is a gift that should be treasured. Moments passed in silent wonder as she stared across the horizon, gaining a new perspective of the landscape and opportunities that awaited at the crest of the next mountain to climb. Before she could take that step, she had to stop and turn back to reach her hand down to help the others get to the top. This view should never be achieved alone and can't fully be appreciated without sharing the journey with others.

Climbing a mountain takes endurance and the tenacity to never give up. The person climbing will face setbacks, storms, and seemingly impossible tasks, but they can still choose to rise. It's at the summit that they will meet a version of themselves they have never known that is stronger, braver, and unshakable.

As much as we think we can be "self-made," the reality lies in the acknowledgment that the highest mountains require a strong Sherpa or *Amiga* to guide the path. I don't believe in the "self-made" person. No one can accomplish great success without the help of other people contributing their gifts and talents toward a common goal. To move forward with hope for a bright future, success is much more attainable when you surround yourself with people who help, not hinder, the process.

Every person has a different definition of success. Over the last twenty-five years, I have regarded the path to success as a journey to undertake, which can be likened to climbing a mountain. No mountain worth climbing is smooth, and it shouldn't be tackled without a strong Sherpa. For centuries, the Sherpas have served as guides, porters, and invaluable companions for mountaineers seeking to scale the world's highest peaks. Their name has become synonymous with resilience, strength, and an intimate understanding of the treacherous mountain landscapes. However, their significance stretches far beyond being mere guides; their contributions extend deeply into the realms of culture, economy, and safety for those who dare to undertake the challenge of these colossal summits.

At the core of their significance lies an unparalleled understanding of the terrain. The Sherpas possess an innate familiarity with the mountains, their weather patterns, crevasses, and precarious routes. This intimate knowledge, passed down through generations, serves as a light of guidance, ensuring the safety and success of mountaineers who entrust themselves to their care. In addition to their unparalleled expertise, Sherpas play an instrumental role in the logistical support required for expeditions. They serve as porters, carrying heavy loads of equipment, food, and supplies, allowing climbers to focus on the climb itself. Their strength and endurance in carrying immense weights through challenging terrain are awe-inspiring, and their unwavering commitment to ensuring the well-being of their climbing parties is unparalleled.

Just like climbing a mountain with the best Sherpa, you need the best teams to build the best path toward your expected goals. I've heard from multiple mentors that you become the average of the five people you spend the most time with. I have been very blessed over the years to be surrounded by many incredible leaders, speakers, mentors, and all-around amazing people. This anthology is dedicated to a core message of how we help others rise as we climb. While I have experienced many ups and downs, these mountain-top and low–valley moments, I have recognized that I have no trouble finding these incredible people. Then I allow life to get in the way. I get distracted by being busy, not productive, and I forget to apply the simple principles that lead to success.

As I found myself circling the mountain of busyness once again, I decided to pause and take stock of how I was investing my time and with whom I was investing it. When reflecting on the powerful friends and mentors I have had, I must take time to honor two women who have had a profound impact on the dramatic shift my life has taken in the last few years. Esmeralda Aharon and Gabriela Ramírez-Arellano are two women who exemplify the values described throughout this book as women who care about helping as many people climb their mountains as they can. They understand we have a limited time here to have an impact, and they are not wasting a moment. I have worked with many people who talk about helping others. I have watched many climb big stages to speak to huge crowds about how to achieve success. When it came time to help me at my low points, I couldn't find many of those people. There were many who *did* help me in my times of need, and I will forever be grateful to those individuals. Words couldn't express how much I valued their help in that time of need. I don't have enough space here to list all of those people, but I want to make sure I take time to honor Esmeralda and Gabriela specifically.

When I was starting my media company, I faced many challenges as I worked tirelessly to build a strong product I could be proud of, attempted to build community through many networks and outreach programs, and invested time and resources to get advertisers to help fund the effort. I spent many sleepless nights staring at the ceiling, trying to come up with creative strategies to drive revenue. An entrepreneur can build incredible products or deliver top-notch service, but without consistent cash flow, they face inevitable bankruptcy and failure. More times than I care to admit, I faced the dreadful monster of failure as I wept over empty bank accounts. I reached out to every network I had. It always surprises me when I am faced with adversity and discover in these moments who will really help. It can be soul-crushing when you discover the individuals who you thought were fighting to help you, only to find out they were plotting your destruction with others in the community.

I will forever remember the day I was ready to quit because I couldn't even pay my cell phone bill. It was going to be shut off later that day, and I had just discovered a community member had pushed their initiative to kill a campaign I had sold to a great company in St. Louis. I was counting on that campaign to keep the company open. I was lost and felt moments of hopelessness. As I humbled myself to reach out in desperation to a few last people, Gabriela answered the call and had her company invest in a campaign that would get the bills paid to keep my company open. She didn't even know how close I was to quitting that day, but it was a moment I will remember forever. When you take an event and tie it to an emotion, it burns in that person's memory. That day is marked on my calendar as another day I didn't quit, but kept moving forward. This got me through until I was in a position to grow the company and one day sell it as a successful venture.

The day I met Esmeralda is also burned in my memory. I was being awarded a tremendous honor with the Hispanic Chamber of St. Louis as the Member of the Year. That night, Esmeralda was being awarded a Lifetime Achievement Award. I sat in awe as I listened to her speech. I remember thinking that this was a woman I needed to meet and better understand how she has been able to achieve so much. Over the last few years, I have been blessed to call her my mentor and *amiga*. Every time we talk, I learn just a little more about her journey. There is not one book, or even a series of books, that could be written to give enough detail about her journey to understand the adversity she has been through and the tenacity required to keep running with the love and empathy she shows to everyone she meets.

As I was beginning a transition period in my life, Gabriela and Esmeralda reached out to me to be a writing coach on their first anthology together, *Calladitas Rising*. I built my media company because I felt that in order for my voice to be heard effectively after 20 years in media, I would have to build my own company. I always wanted to be a writer, but was consistently pushed into the sales divisions. I could never get my voice heard. Gabriela and Esmeralda didn't know that I was sitting on a children's book that I hadn't been able to finish since 2007, or other books that I haven't been able to write since my first anthology in 2017. Helping with that project, hearing the stories of the incredible women, and understanding how they overcame their struggles created a space for me to break out of my shell. This launched my hope and belief in the ability for me to be able to do the things that once seemed so impossible. Again, I come back to the power of those you surround yourself with. Spending time with champions who believe in you and lift you up when you feel broken can change everything. Sometimes, we just need the encouragement. Sometimes, we need more practical solutions to get past difficult circumstances. Again, I am so thankful for every "Sherpa" who has helped in my journey. Now it's time to give back.

A Sherpa doesn't carry someone up the mountain, they walk beside them, guiding the way. They know every twist in the trail, when to push forward, when to pause, and where the footing is strongest. The climber still has to take each step, face the altitude, and endure the climb, but the Sherpa ensures they don't do it alone. With quiet strength and hard-earned wisdom, the Sherpa helps others reach heights they may never have believed possible.

Amigas, take time to identify your Sherpas. When you've reached that mountaintop, pause to enjoy the view, then look back with your arms extended to help our sisters climb with you.

Together, we rise, mis amigas!

(Note: The underlying story for this chapter originally appeared in the Holiday Gift Guide for the Collinsville Daily News in 2023.)

Jackie Duty is a Chilean-American visionary leader, author, speaker, and marketing consultant with a 20-year career in corporate media, spanning newspapers, radio, television, magazines, and digital technologies. She now serves as the executive director of ThriVe® Metro East, a nonprofit organization dedicated to providing life-affirming care to women during their most critical moments.

Before joining ThriVe, Jackie launched her own marketing agency and online media company, which was read in 155 countries, helping businesses and nonprofits share their stories with impact. She is a passionate advocate for purpose-driven leadership and leverages storytelling and the arts to empower individuals and communities. She has helped multiple companies launch in the retail, mobile, restaurant, and hospitality industries, including an art gallery.

Jackie is driven by her mission to help others rise—whether by empowering women to choose life, honoring veterans' legacies, or mentoring creatives and entrepreneurs to find their voice and walk boldly in their purpose.

Please scan the QR code to connect with this author.

Afterword

Finding comPASSION in commUNITY

"There are those too gentle to live among wolves."
— Alan Watts

...and those too generous of spirit to allow the gentle among
us to succumb to a virus.

(Note: I originally wrote the core of this chapter as a blog on March 16, 2020. The world had shut down just four days prior, due to the pandemic. As I recently began writing my chapter for "Amigas," the words I found myself typing sounded very familiar, and the more I typed, the more I realized I was repeating myself, and the memory of my original blog flashed in my brain. What follows is an expanded version of that original blog.)

It's time. We are all here on this planet, at this particular time, for a definite reason, and our job is to stand up, speak up, and lift up—not to sit back and watch.

You see, there is a **V.I.R.U.S.** among us. This **Violent, Irrational, Relentless, Undesirable, Situation** has developed into global chaos with an outcome solely dependent on our reaction to it. In the beginning, its impact was downplayed as "nothing to worry about…it will be gone before we know it." Yet, this VIRUS has a rampant viral insensitivity, knows no boundaries, and takes all as prisoners. What started as a little something we could once ignore and hide from has now exploded into an uncontrollable beast, of which even the highest spiritual counsel on the planet can only pray for a cure.

The VIRUS I'm describing is a lack of compassion, a lack of community.

What happened to our empathy, our sense of caring? When did we forget how to play well together in the sandbox and to stand up together against bullies? It has all been replaced by the nonsense of division and entitlement.

It's time for each of us to claim ownership of our contribution to the growth of this VIRUS, not just focus on survival. When we succumb to anger, isolation, and fear, the VIRUS grows. The macro (planet) is only a reflection of the micro (you and me). The tornadoes, storms, fires, earthquakes, and floods (macro) are all reflections of the negative energy being produced by the current insanity of humanity (micro). We cannot wait for the "bigger brick" to hit us upside the head. There is no bigger brick… the VIRUS *is* the frickin' bigger brick.

We start thinking that everyone is "out to get us," and we feel compelled to either hide and/or over-protect our own little corner of the world, which is exactly how the VIRUS grows. The answer is not to hide or lash out in anger—that only creates division. Our defenses rise when we lose our sense of empathy and compassion. Yet when we gather and bond as a community, it's much easier to defeat the VIRUS.

Answers lie within each of us as we stand up, speak up, and reclaim our power. The VIRUS wants us to feel powerless and fearful, which only fuels its sense of grandeur and makes it feel more omnipotent. Many people feel that so much in life is out of our control right now, yet perhaps this negative VIRUS is actually handing us the opportunity to focus on what we *can* control—ourselves and our reactions. When we turn our focus away from the VIRUS, it begins to shrink, wither, and worry. When we turn IN-ward...inside our own mind, body, and spiritual connection...inside our closest circle of family, friends, and colleagues...we no longer need the VIRUS. We do not need, nor want, to live in the shadow of fear. As we move out of fear, we take back our power.

We are at a crucial tipping point.

Now is the time for each of us to re-ignite the flames of compassion and community and empower one another. Please take care of what you need to at home, then remember to take care of your community. We all speak about compassion, and we all say we want to help, but quite often we let other people do the work or we keep quiet so as not to draw attention or rock the boat. This is not the time to sit back with a wait-and-see attitude. That party is over.

What can we do in our own little micro-world, now?

- We can clean up, repair, or "fix" within our own sphere of influence, *now*.

- Whatever we have put on the back burner to "deal with later" needs our attention, *now*.

- Watch out for those who need us; reach out with our help (time, talent, treasure), *now*.

- How can we extend a hand and be the "lift" someone else needs, right *now*?

We need compassion and community.

We need each other. The planet needs you and me. *People* need you and me, and we need them. My guess is that you have probably already noticed the abundance of helpers and healers who have heard the call, identified their gift, and are offering their services—educators, trainers, speakers, motivational coaches, life coaches, business coaches, communication coaches, spiritual coaches, emotional intelligence coaches, health coaches, leadership coaches, relationship coaches, psychiatrists, therapists, nurses, doctors, and more (oh my!). You name it, and there is probably a coach for it. At first, this might seem intimidating (especially if you are in the same line of business), but I see it as a blessing.

I believe there is an invisible power for good at the helm, and these Helpers and Healers—**you, me, them**—are here, on purpose, at this specific time in history. These are the people whose life paths have become their hero's journey. It is through this extensive training that they have inadvertently formed an invisible "safety net" in preparation to help the planet heal, transform, and thrive. This is our job, our purpose, our mission.

Waiting, watching, wondering.

It's time. We've been called to step up, find our voice, share our wisdom, and be part of the solution. We are here as authors, collaborators, and partners. The strength of our safety net lies in our numbers and our ability to create strong connections and strong communities.

Every aspect of our existence (environment, politics, health, race, religion, education, gender identification, immigration, relationships, business, finance, etc.) has been turned upside down, tossed into a gigantic jar of muddy water...shaken **and** stirred. We are **all** now sitting on the universal planetary shelf, in a jar of muddy water, just waiting for things to settle, watching for clarity, and constantly wondering what the H#@L is going to happen next.

Muddy water.
Sitting still.
Gets clear.

As we sit and wait, the silt begins to settle, and we can see our next step more clearly. That's where *we* come in. *We* are going to happen next. *We* are going to step up. Many of you already have. Your passion and dedication to your work, mission, and message put you at the forefront of change! Your willingness to step up, use your voice, volunteer, gather in community, share your opinion in public, and take the initiative to donate or lend a hand to help pave the way with courage and hope for the rest of us.

Do it now. Reach out. Extend a helping hand. Volunteer to be another thread of hope in someone's safety net.

- Remember what it was like to sit on your front porch, get to know your neighbors, and ask what they needed help with? Go do that.

- Haven't seen your neighbor across the street in a while? It's time to check in and make sure everything is all right in their world.

- If all you can muster right now is to watch, learn, and be someone else's cheerleader, then please do that.

Then, when it's time, go *get involved*; make some *good trouble*. Because, together, I believe we can create a more caring, compassionate, and giving global community, whether it's next door, around the corner, or around the world.

–Cathy Davis
Founder and CEO, Davis Creative, LLC

Cathy Davis founded Davis Creative, LLC, in January 2004, as a creative branding services agency. In 2008, she expanded her services to include publishing. Today, the Davis Creative Publishing division is a recognized industry leader, having helped over 2,000 authors become published and over 700 authors achieve Amazon Best Seller status, including more than 45 anthologies. Cathy believes it's when we share our wisdom through our stories that we make a difference in the lives of others.

Besides being a businesswoman, Cathy is a trustee member with Forest Park Forever and volunteers with the National Council of Jewish Women (NCJW). She previously served on the board of the St. Louis chapter of the National Speakers Association (NSA), where she still contributes as an instructor, and is a former co-dean of the STL Speaker's Academy. Cathy lives in St. Louis, MO, with her husband, Jack, and their rescue SchnickerDoodle, Chewy (AKA: Chief Barketing Director).

Please scan the QR code to connect with this author.

DavisCreativePublishing.com

We empower thought leaders and transformational coaches to publish books that engage their audience, enhance their credibility, and inspire positive change.

 davis creative PUBLISHING

GHOST PUBLISHERS OF SOLO BOOKS & ANTHOLOGIES